Dramatizing Mother Goose

Introducing Students to Classic Literature through Drama

TO MY MOTHER, JOSEPHINE HORGAN THISTLE,
WHO SHOWED ME HOW TO PERSIST.
SHE LOVED BEAUTY AND THE PLAY OF THE IMAGINATION,
AND GAVE ME THE GIFT OF HER CHILDLIKE HEART.

Published by Smith and Kraus, Inc.
PO Box 127, Lyme, NH 03768
Copyright ©1998 by Louise Thistle
Manufactured in the United States of America

Cover and Text Design by Julia Hill
Illustrations by Emily Packer, Susan Corey, and Louise Thistle

First Edition: January 1998
10 9 8 7 6 5 4 3 2 1

The Library of Congress Cataloging-In-Publication Data
Thistle, Louise.
Dramatizing Mother Goose: introducing students
to classic literature through drama / Louise Thistle. —1st ed.
p.   cm.   — (Young actors series)
Includes bibliographical references and indexes.
ISBN 1-57525-125-6
1. Drama in education. I. Title. II. Series.
PN3171.T48   1997
317.39'9—dc21   97-26709
CIP

Dramatizing Mother Goose

Introducing Students to Classic Literature through Drama

Louise Thistle

Young Actors Series

A Smith and Kraus Book

Smith and Kraus
Young Actors Series

If you would like prepublication information about upcoming Smith and Kraus books, you may receive our semiannual catalogue, free of charge, by sending your name and address to Smith and Kraus Catalogue, PO Box 127, Lyme, NH 03768. Or call (800) 895-4331.

CONTENTS

ACKNOWLEDGMENTS

I want to thank the many people who made this book possible. First, I thank my mother, to whom this book is dedicated. Next, I thank Emily Packer who spent hours helping on every aspect of it from proofreading to decisions on content and on the drawing of the many pictures.

I thank Mary Ann Petteway, who read the manuscript several times. Her sensitivity to words and literature greatly enhanced its writing style. I thank Dianne Tucker-La Plount, whose painstaking copyediting helped make the material clear and accessible for teachers. I appreciate the advice of Jenny Hartman, whose excellent taste in art and literature enriches all of my work. Sharon Oppenheimer, Ph.D., continues to offer imaginative practical ideas on ways to help teachers dramatize with students.

Jo Ann Takemoto field-tested each dramatization in her classroom. Her students gave me wonderful suggestions for gestures. Mrs. Takemoto also gave me valuable editorial suggestions and helped me dramatize the rhymes in a family literacy event, proving the power of the rhymes to enchant people of all ages.

Susan Longstaff's fourth graders were the first to teach the dramatizations to other students by traveling to different classes and presenting their dramatizations to them. Claudia Leonesio-Mons explained how she used the rhymes to teach effective stage speech. Demetrice Davis described how she used the rhymes to teach middle school students heightened stage speech.

Ruth Burgess, Director of the London Workshop Company, helped develop improvisations based on the rhymes. She showed me, by example, the power of improvisations to motivate students. Bonnie McGrath gave me helpful ideas on pantomiming the rhymes and suggested ways to use the rhymes to develop reading and writing. Susan More field-tested the Miss Muffet dramatization with her first graders.

Ona Russell was the first to suggest using the rhymes to teach writing and literature appreciation to college students. Salley Deaton explained how she would use the political rhymes in her college business classes.

For help with the art and graphics, I thank Dudley Hartman, who designed the Dramatic Action Picture Page. Peggy Wolter added enlivening artistic touches to the pictures.

Richard Holborow and Diane Wilson of the Copy Hut in Ocean Beach gave expert care and attention to my many copying needs.

I thank the patrons of the Newbreak Coffee House in Ocean Beach who have helped me. Among them is Negar Khodadeh who offered enthusiasm and reinforcement throughout the project.

Rex Riley provided me with graphic help. Becky Riley and the Riley's daughter Katherine field-tested my dramatizations and gave me immediate feedback. Daniel Toporski provides continual generous computer help and advice. Lance Murphy offers on-the-spot support in times of computer crisis.

Ray Blavatt gave me invaluable tips on book design and cartoon animation. Kathy Blavatt provided expert suggestions on page layout and design. Bobbie Silverman gave me ideas on delicate artistic details. Jolie Kalfian generously created the prototype of the Dramatic Action Picture Page. Lisa Unamuno was influential in the cover design.

I especially thank Newbreak Coffee Company owner Norma Slaaman, her daughter, Andrea, and the other hosts at the shop for providing the community with excellent food and coffee and an inviting and inspiring place for the community to meet.

Camille Kalinger enthusiastically promotes literature dramatization. Meigs Ingham, Manager of the Old Globe Gift Shop in San Diego, has helped introduce literature dramatization to hundreds of teachers.

I thank my dad, Lewis Thistle, who imbued me with a love of the classics. I thank Sylvan Barnet, my first literature and writing teacher at Tufts University. His appreciation of great literature and his profound down-to-earth way of analyzing it have influenced me throughout my life. I thank Jack Sanford whose wisdom and guidance have been fundamental in my work. His belief in the importance of "the development of the imagination as the source of all creativity" guides my work.

Finally, I thank my husband Charles who provides both editorial and emotional support. The manuscript would not be nearly as effective and accessible for teachers if it weren't for his skillful editorial guidance. Of course, we both appreciate evenings with our faithful lap cat, Bell.

Louise Thistle

INTRODUCTION

This book develops language and literature through drama. It is a truism that the more involved you are in a subject or activity the more meaningful and exciting it becomes. By reciting and dramatizing every line in classic Mother Goose rhymes, students experience the language and literature in an exciting, purposeful way.

Dramatizing Mother Goose has been evolving for more than twelve years. I had agreed to teach poetry dramatization to students of all ethnic and socioeconomic backgrounds and academic abilities as well as English learners.

I needed material that would plunge them immediately into dramatization, and that would efficiently teach them good speaking skills. I needed excellent literature to involve the students and to develop reading, language, and literature appreciation.

I landed on Mother Goose rhymes because there's an action to do in every line. I found its nonsense verse appealing because of its playful use of language, opportunity to make vocalized sound effects, and its encouragement of students themselves becoming the inanimate objects. Nonsense Verse also, of course, has imaginative characters and actions that are inviting to dramatize.

The rhymes are short and musical. Students know them or can easily memorize them so acting students can focus on practicing speaking skills rather than having to read with their heads buried in a book. Older students and adults became interested in the rhymes when they learned that the rhymes were originally composed 200 years ago to entertain grown-ups.

The rhymes are also an important part of our cultural literary heritage. *The Dictionary of Cultural Literacy* by E. D. Hirsch et al. mentions fifteen rhymes dramatized in this book that everyone should be familiar with to be considered culturally literate.

I have found people of all ages and backgrounds, including English learners, have enjoyed dramatizing them. This is because the rhymes come from the oral tradition and were meant for reciting and dramatizing.

They are also full of imagination, the source of all creativity. Students hunger to use their imaginations in this dynamic way. Increasingly, educators and psychologists have become concerned that TV, video games, and computers are deadening the imagination of young people by handing the images to them. This makes them passive.

"The imagination is the core of who we are," said Maria Anagnostopoulos, educational director of The Greek Institute. "Tapping into our imaginations takes a person to the creative source, to life itself." Dramatization gives people a feeling of creative empowerment. No one is passive. Everyone acts the rhyme—recreating it in an imaginative way.

As one teacher said, the rhymes epitomize the play of the imagination. "Everything about them is imaginative," she said, "the unusual use of language, the characters, the little scenes they paint, and the unexpected endings. This imaginative quality is perhaps why many artists over the centuries have wanted to illustrate them."

As I worked with the rhymes, I saw the value of focusing intently on each line of a rhyme to develop both dramatization and literature and language appreciation. As I dramatized the rhymes with students, teachers and students showed me how to use the rhymes to serve diverse needs.

Dramatization, of course, uses what Harvard psychologist Howard Gardner describes as "multiple intelligences." Dramatization uses linguistic, bodily-kinesthetic, musical, intrapersonal (self-awareness), interpersonal, and spatial intelligences.

"The more ways students interact with academic material, the more exciting and meaningful it is," said a second grade teacher. The incorporating of multiple intelligences gives all students the opportunity to feel involved and comfortable. At the same time, dramatization develops all of the intelligences in a pleasurable way.

Teachers of English language told me that the rhymes' brevity, action, and vivid word pictures make them non-threatening and enjoyable to English learners. Since the rhymes are musical and epitomize the cadence of English speech, they imbue these students with English in a pleasant way.

A special education teacher found the dramatization offered a creative vent for students with difficulties in reading and writing. "The dramatization gives active expression for the body," he said. "It also gives students, who feel left out during the regular curriculum, the chance to be creative. Students with Attention Deficit Disorder benefit from doing the exuberant actions with artistic controlled movements."

Reciting and then reading Mother Goose rhymes teaches children to read. In a *New York Times* article, Gina Kolata wrote that "rhymes may train the brain by having children focus on the intonation and matching sounds. Children hear the sounds, and so when they later see the words in print, they can read them."

Literature and drama teachers of upper-grade students have also used the rhymes. Dr. Barbara Schuch, an English-Social Studies teacher of middle school gifted students, has students study the rhymes' historical background and uses them as an introduction to the study of nonsense verse.

Claudia Leonesio-Mons, drama specialist at the Vista Academy of Visual and Performing Arts, found that the rhymes were effective material in teaching projection and other stage speaking skills because they are short and full of action. She said students know them or can memorize them quickly. Thus, they can focus on gesturing and speaking loudly and clearly.

This book uses a method called "Expressive Gesture" dramatization. The technique involves participants doing expressive gestures as they recite and dramatize each line of a rhyme. Field testing revealed that this method involved people of all ages and language and academic backgrounds quickly and enthusiastically in the drama.

Techniques of formalized expressive gesturing are, of course, used in many theatrical traditions. Gestures representing certain feelings and actions are the basis of traditional Japanese Kabuki theatre, the commedia dell'arte, slapstick comedy, silent screen acting, and the dramatizations of such traditional cultures as the Native Americans and the Balinese.

Teachers requested that I provide gestures to enact each line in a rhyme. Naturally, individuals will execute the gestures in their own way, and imagination and artistry come in the way the gestures are done. Of course, too, the gestures provided are suggestions, and teachers and students may well want to create their own gestures. Indeed, student gestures are often more spontaneous and apropos and make the expression their own.

This book also describes activities using "Process Drama" or improvisational drama. In "Process Drama," students create their own dialogue and interpretations based on the rhymes. The approach, for example, can be done with the "Leader in Role" in which the teacher (or other leader) plays a role and interacts with the students.

What has touched me most while dramatizing the rhymes in classrooms, community centers, and libraries is that all can succeed and benefit from dramatizing them. There is little material available that is excellent literature and still accessible, profitable, and enjoyable to such a wide spectrum of people.

Using *Dramatizing Mother Goose* in the Classroom

CHAPTER 1 explains three acting principles students should follow. Following these principles helps students get fully involved in the literature and language and teaches them acting skills.

CHAPTER 2 explains four principles of effective stage and public speech. Using these principles will involve students in the language and literature making it active, understandable, and enjoyable to English learners. Practicing the principles also trains students in good stage and public speech.

CHAPTER 3 gives techniques to inspire dramatization. A section is devoted to methods to develop language through drama for English learners. This chapter also describes methods and activities using improvisation and pantomime.

CHAPTER 4 describes how to incorporate commercial or homemade instruments and simple costume pieces and fabrics.

CHAPTER 5 is a model introductory lesson in poetry dramatization. It uses the rhyme, "Little Miss Muffet," as the central example in a first lesson that has been used with modifications with all age levels and English learners.

CHAPTER 6 is the heart of the book. It contains 17 of the most popular Mother Goose Rhymes dramatized. Each rhyme has three pages devoted to it.

CHAPTER 7 gives historical background on the origin of the figure of Mother Goose and on each of the dramatized rhymes.

CHAPTER 8 discusses the rhymes as literature. Using "Jack and Jill" as a prototype, it describes the poetic conventions used in many of the rhymes. It includes comments by writers and a psychologist on their literary significance and value for students.

CHAPTER 9 has suggested literature questions and other activities based on the rhymes.

The book has two indexes. An Activity Level Index indicates if they are "Quieting," "Moderately Active," or "Active" to help teachers use them to set different moods. The Subject Index lists the rhymes in categories such as Animals, Farming, Adults, and Children as an aid to use them with other areas of the curriculum.

An Annotated Bibliography lists noteworthy Mother Goose picture books and scholarly books on the history and literary background of Mother Goose. It also has books on creative drama, costuming, and books and resources on making and obtaining rhythm instruments.

An Appendix has a copy of the book's seventeen rhymes to use for group or pair dramatizations.

Dramatizing Mother Goose

Introducing Students to Classic Literature through Drama

CHAPTER ONE

The Three Principles of Good Acting

Three simple principles are the foundation of a good acting program:

Believe you are the part you are playing.

Exercise **control** over your actions and emotions.

Use **voice and movement** expressively.

These principles are followed by all good actors. If students practice them, their acting will be successful. Involvement with the language and literature will be deep and satisfying. The experience will be rewarding for all concerned.

Children from preschool to grade two do not benefit from a lengthy discussion of the principles. Younger children need only to be told to make believe, to use control, and to show the character's feelings with their voices and bodies. They should often be commended for doing these things.

Students grade three and above benefit greatly from knowing and focusing on these acting techniques. It teaches them about the art of acting and can be what makes the experience particularly interesting and rewarding to them.

For readers, list the principles on the board or a chart and refer to them throughout any lesson. If students get off track, it is usually because they are not following one or more of the principles.

BELIEF

Tell students that believing or fully pretending to be the characters they are playing is essential. The more they are able and willing to believe that they are inside the shoes of a character or the fur or feathers of an animal, the more dynamic and involving the experience will be. For example, if a student plays a bouncy dog, she or he must pretend to get inside the skin of that dog and be the dog with short lively legs, big panting tongue, and floppy active ears. If someone plays an arrogant queen, she must imagine that she is the center of the universe and her pleasures are her sole concern.

To inspire belief:

- Discuss with students the need to believe in the parts they're playing to make the drama come alive. Refer to the film, *The Wizard of Oz,* pointing out how 17-year-old Judy Garland pretended to be a little girl and how other actors became a wicked witch, a man of tin, a cowardly lion and a man of straw. This film is a good example because it shows students that adults use their imagination and act in children's plays.

- Show the "Developing Drama and Language" pictures from Chapter Six and pictures from other books to help students climb inside the characters that they will play.

- Model belief. For example, when acting "Little Jack Horner," bow perkily as the spunky boy; turn definitely to sit in your corner; make eager, big biting, and chewing motions enjoying every bit of your pie. Your enthusiastic dramatizing will inspire theirs.

- Continually reinforce students' believable acting. Smile and interact with those participating fully. After each dramatization, point out the students who are putting effort and imagination into, for example, becoming a fierce North wind, a hungry dog, or a twinkling star.

- Use students' spontaneous gestures. For example, if a student twists around or bends down to become a fierce wind, do it too. If someone strokes her hair as a haughty queen, follow her example. The imitation of their actions will inspire more gestures and spontaneous actions from them.

- When an acting assignment is evaluated, ask students to focus on which actors seemed to believe the parts they were playing, and what they did specifically to make it seem real.

CONTROL

A legitimate teacher concern is that students will get out of control when acting. A good definition of art in general is giving form and focus to strong feelings and emotions. Control gives drama artistry and purpose. Exercising artistic control also brings a feeling of accomplishment. Exercising control is essential to successful, satisfying classroom dramatization for all concerned.

To help instill and maintain control:

- Discuss the need to exercise control to make the drama artistic and worthwhile. For older students, explain how theater and film actors use controlled, stylized actions that have been practiced and sometimes choreographed when they fight, leap, push and carry out other aggressive actions.

- Use the "freeze" technique to begin and end each rhyme's dramatization. For example, begin "Little Jack Horner" with Jack "frozen" in midst of his bow. End it in a frozen picture with him holding out imaginary suspenders. The freeze technique is a freqent device used by directors to begin and end a scene or play.

- Slow down the rate of your own speech, and use a low calm voice to slow down students' actions. This technique is most helpful when the drama is getting too emotional and exuberant.

- Have students act "in place" traveling actions, such as running, climbing up hills, prancing and skipping.

- Model using slow motion and enlarged gestures when doing actions, such as, becoming the blowing North wind, the falling snow, the "three bags full."

- Use voiceless yells for such things as Little Miss Muffet's scream or Humpty's fall, capturing the expression with the body and face only.

- Do falls in slow motion. For example, have Humpty fall off a high wall to slow down the rate of the action. Say F - A - L - L slowly, elongating the word to accommodate his slow, long drop.

- Use a control device, such as a bell, to begin acting and to end it. For example, say, "When I ring the bell, take the position of the character at the beginning of the rhyme. When I ring the bell at the end, freeze in the position of the character in the final action of the rhyme."

- After dramatizing a rhyme, gesture and say rhythmically and emphatically, "SIT DOWN," to get students focused and ready to listen or to dramatize another rhyme.

- Use peer evaluation to point out times when control was good or to discuss what students might do to exercise more control.

- Encourage students to stand on two feet to play animals, as they are portraying both an animal and a character, and can maneuver better. (Preschoolers may feel more comfortable crawling. Allow them to do so.)

- End dramatization sessions with a Quieting Rhyme, such as "Twinkle,

Twinkle, Little Star." (See the Index in which such rhymes are indicated).
Or, have students illustrate and write about their favorite rhyme.

VOICE AND MOVEMENT

Voice and movement means using different kinds of voices, body movements, and gestures to portray different characters, their actions, and their feelings. These are the tools with which actors portray their parts.

The characters in Mother Goose rhymes are broad types giving opportunity to use expressive voice and movement. For example, a huge Humpty egg would use a big, full voice and wobble bulkily from side to side. A twinkling star, in contrast, would use a light, delicate voice and quick, flexible actions.

To teach voice and movement:

- Have students practice using the voice and movement of two contrasting characters. For example, say, "GO AWAY," first as a big, resonant grandfather clock, and then say *Go away,"* as the tiny mouse going up it.

- Model using an expressive voice and movement to portray these types. For example, be overly sprightly and enthusiastic as you recite "Jack be Nimble." Spin with exaggerated "nimble" vitality to portray his agile movements. Or, bend over, shake a hand, and hobble feebly as Mother Hubbard using a quavering voice as you recite her attempt to locate a bone.

- Let individuals demonstrate their dramatic interpretations. Reinforce expressiveness, such as a pompously saluting Duke of York with chest and head thrust out or a desperately anxious Bo-Peep searching wide-eyed for her lost sheep.

- Invite students participating wholeheartedly with voice and movement to dramatize with you at the front of the room. Their committed acting will inspire the acting of the other students.

CHAPTER TWO

The Four Principles of Effective Stage Speech

Four speaking principles create dynamic speech that will make literature and language come alive. These principles are followed by all good actors and effective public speakers. The principles are:

Projection: speaking loudly enough so that every word is heard.

Articulation: speaking all letters in a word distinctly so that the exact word is clear.

Colorization: coloring your speech so that words sound like what they describe.

Slowing the pace: slowing the rate of speech to focus on each important word and phrase.

American speech tends to be flat and rushed and trail off at the end of sentences. Students profit greatly from practicing principles that correct these faults and bring vitality into speech. Practicing these principles also helps them fully and sensually experience both the earthiness and the magic of the language and literature spoken.

The practice of these principles is particularly beneficial to language learners, helping them understand, enjoy, and participate in a new language.

Practicing these principles also trains students in the techniques necessary to deliver an effective speech, an ability important in all professions.

Students as young as preschool profit from following these principles. Students grades two and below, however, will learn the techniques of good speaking best by your modeling, encouraging, and reinforcing them continually in an informal way. You might, for example, say, "We need to speak loudly so everyone can enjoy what we're saying." Or, "I liked how slowly and clearly you spoke. I understood every word."

For readers, list the principles on the board or a chart and refer to them throughout any lesson. A detailed description of how to introduce and teach the principles is in Chapter Five, "A Model Lesson."

PROJECTION

Projection means throwing your voice out to the back of a space so that everyone can hear what you're saying. Projection is the first and most important principle. If students project well, they are involved in the material and are putting energy into their speech. Most students do not project well, and it requires continual training effort.

To instill good projection:

- Have students define projection. Ask what happens to an audience if speakers or actors don't project.

- Mention that the most important requirement of an actor is a strong flexible voice. Add that, when directing a play, many directors first look for actors who are able to project their voices.

- Explain that in the early days of theatre, there were no microphones and actors had to project to the back of large auditoriums.

- Model poor and then good projection. Invite a student to the front of the room and carry on a brief conversation about the weather—first using poor and then good projection. Ask which conversation would be more interesting to an audience and why.

- Practice projection with students—mentioning first that it requires using a strong voice and doesn't involve shouting which would annoy an audience. Then, have students stand and chant "**PROJECTION**" four times while at the same time making a clear projecting or tossing motion (as if throwing out a ball) to the opposite end of the room.

- Always reject poor projection. Push for better projection by, if necessary, continually interrupting and saying "louder" when it's missing. Praise improvement and coax poor projectors to attain a higher level.

- Emphasize the need for good projection each time students read aloud and always reinforce it when it's accomplished.

ARTICULATION

Articulation means saying every letter in words distinctly so the exact word is understood. For example, "cat," sounds like "cat" and not "cab" or "can."

Good articulation brings clarity and energy into speech. It requires paying meticulous attention to each word spoken. British speakers often use excellent articulation. Precise articulation is essential in reciting poetry in which every word counts and should be absolutely clear.

To help instill good articulation:

- Model poor and then good articulation. For example, say "cat" swallowing the "t." Say it again emphasizing the "t." Ask students to describe the difference the second time you said it.

- Ask why poetry recitation demands exceptional articulation.

- Practice using good diction with them. Have them rise and chant "**AR TIC U LA TION**" four times pointing emphatically at each syllable with an index finger to dramatize enunciating each syllable clearly.

- Articulate words from rhymes, such as "cow," "moon," "jumped," "sport." Then, recite the whole rhyme focusing on using good articulation.

- Let students choose rhymes to recite concentrating on using good articulation.

COLORIZATION

Colorization means saying words so they sound like what they describe and, when possible, making dramatic gestures to illustrate them. For example, "nimble" can be made to sound light and nimble; "tiny" can be made to sound "tiny." It is a distinctive technique of storytellers and actors to help audiences experience the action and imagery of a poem or story.

To develop the technique of colorization:

- Ask students what it means that speakers should speak colorfully when reciting poetry. Make a big colorful gesture as you say "colorfully" in a colorful voice.

- Have students rise and chant "**COLORIZATION**" four times, each time opening their arms out in a big, wide, colorful gesture.

- Recite a rhyme focusing on using colorful speech to express the words' meaning. For example, recite "Humpty Dumpty" in a big, full voice. Say, "Sat on a wall," heavily. Stretch out "F-A-L-L" as he plummets off a high wall. Add excitement and speed up the pace as the horsemen prance during "all the king's horses, and all the king's men." Slow down your speech and shrug hopelessly on "Couldn't put Humpty together again."

- Let students choose rhymes to recite line by line making each word as colorful as possible.

SLOWING THE PACE

Slowing the rate of speech and the pace of gestures is an artistic control device. In our speeded up society, it requires discipline to slow the pace. One of the most annoying traits of poor public speakers is speaking too fast from nervousness or from feeling rushed.

Drama and the recitation of poetry or any literature should never be rushed. Slowing the rate helps participants and the audience concentrate on every important word and line of a poem.

A slow pace also helps participants experience the language sensually, on the lips, teeth, tongue, and palate. Speakers are often struck at how attentively audiences respond when they slow down the rate of speech and create big, slow gestures. It is an antidote to our too fast-paced society.

To instill slowing the pace:

- Model a slow rate of speech and action yourself. For example, when introducing a lesson, slow the rate of your motions as you hold a triangle high; tap it three times, taking time to turn and face toward the audience at the left, right and center of the room; make a slow, large, welcoming gesture with your arms, and freeze, demonstrating artistic control.

- Ask students why it's important to recite poetry slowly.

- Model a too-speedy delivery of a rhyme and then a slowed-down version. Ask students which an audience would prefer and why.

- Have students stand and chant with you, "**SLOW-THE-PACE**" four times, each time slowly opening arms out to your sides to emphasize each word and a slow rate of speech.

- Consciously enlarge and slow down your gestures and your recitation of the rhymes.

- Let students choose a rhyme to recite focusing on slowing the pace. Recite and dramatize it with slowed-down gestures, as if making a film in slow motion.

CHAPTER THREE

Techniques to Inspire Dramatization

This chapter contains tips on how to set up the classroom and teach the lesson to inspire the most involved dramatization from students.

DEVELOPING THE IMAGINATION

The central goal of literature dramatization is the development of the imagination.
    Older elementary school students and upper grade students in particular yearn for opportunities to express their imaginations and to be reinforced for it. Older students may be reluctant to dramatize at first feeling "it's not cool" or that they will look silly to peers.

The following techniques help foster and develop students' imaginations:

- For students grades three and above, discuss actors they admire. Mention that great actors of all ages use their imaginations. Refer to the film "The Wizard of Oz" in which adults play a little girl, a scarecrow, a lion, and a man of steel.

- Mention that actors often begin their careers by acting in children's plays. Point out that British actors have acted Mother Goose rhymes on the stage.

- Model using the imagination yourself. For example, "baa" heartily as Baa, Baa, Black Sheep and hobble feebly as Mother Hubbard. Your playful behavior will inspire theirs. Your participation too creates an imaginative bond with the class that lasts long after the lesson is through.

- Continually praise and reinforce those participating. If only two or three eighth graders participate at first, focus on them, interact with them, and verbally reinforce their "wonderful use of imagination." Invite eager participants to the front of the room to dramatize with you.

• Most importantly, use students' imaginative suggestions. For example, if a kindergarten girl suggests putting fingers through imaginary suspenders as Jack Horner saying, "What a good boy am I?," immediately try her "good idea." If a sixth grade boy suggests that a king get his bags of gold from a vault, have him demonstrate opening the vault, and you do it too. If two middle school girls want to become the curtain opening and closing to begin and end the drama, incorporate their "inventive suggestion." Mother Goose rhymes with their inventiveness invite all types of playful interpretations.

• The more excitement the teacher shows for student input, the more students' ideas will come forth. This, of course, enriches the dramatization for all concerned, making it truly a collaborative effort.

VISUAL AIDS

Pictures stimulate the imagination. Examining pictures of the characters helps students climb inside the characters and their situations. For example, have them look at a picture of Miss Muffet running off from a tiny spider, her long ringlets bouncing and her petticoats flying. The picture helps students focus on the character and project into the situation. Pictures loosen inhibitions and self-consciousness, helping students focus on the characters, rather than on themselves.

The Developing Drama and Language picture page with each rhyme in this book shows the characters in costume and action. Students can study and discuss these pictures. They might recreate the actions in "frozen pictures." Students also profit from examining illustrations from other Mother Goose books. (See Bibliography).

OTHER METHODS TO DRAMATIZE LITERATURE USING MOTHER GOOSE

PANTOMIME

Students love action. Good pantomime expresses a characters' actions and feelings clearly through movement and facial expression without using words. Pantomime is enlivening to do and to observe. It teaches the acting skill of communicating without words. Everyone can understand the story using this ancient form of expression. Some pantomime activities follow.

Mime a Rhyme

In "Mime a Rhyme," students pantomime a rhyme with the goal of showing each line's meaning through movement and without using words. To promote clear movements, groups or pairs choose a rhyme, (using the "Mother Goose Rhymes To Dramatize or Pantomime" page in the Appendix) and practice miming it.

After five minutes or so of preparation (a short time focuses creativity), groups present their mimes to the class. The goal is to present movements clearly so that the audience can easily guess the rhyme. The audience guesses, however, after the rhyme has been fully dramatized to honor the presentation. Finally, the class comments on which specifics were done that clearly communicated the characters' feelings and actions.

Frozen Picture Scenes

Many Mother Goose rhymes are stories or scenes with a beginning, middle, and end. Frozen picture scenes teach the concept of beginning, middle, and ending scenes in a story or play. The activity also teaches the acting technique of using heightened expression to show the essence of the action.

To create frozen picture scenes, students in groups pick a rhyme and determine the beginning, middle, and ending actions and create them in "still pictures." For example, in "Little Jack Horner," the first scene might be a frozen picture of Jack's sitting in a corner and eating; the second, Jack pulling out the plum; and the third, his standing with plum in the air.

IMPROVISATION

Improvisation means creating dialogue and sometimes the characters and situations in a drama "on the spot" without using a script. It is "Process Drama" because the participants are involved in the process of creating the drama.

Actors often use improvisations to explore characters' motivations. Students enjoy doing improvisations because they are spontaneous and their own creation.

Teacher In Role

"Teacher in role" is an improvisational device in which the teacher or another adult plays a role in the drama. The teacher, for example, might play a TV interviewer and question the students playing Mother Goose characters on what happened to them in a rhyme.

"Teacher in role" develops and reinforces the value of the imagination. Older students are often more willing to take a risk and participate when they see the teacher playing the theatre game.

The following describes some improvisational activities.

Celebrity Interview

In the celebrity interview, the interviewer (either the teacher-in-role or a student) questions celebrity guests (in this case, Mother Goose characters) about their experiences. Questions might be factual, such as, "Mother Hubbard, why did you go to the cupboard?" or "Boy Blue, where were you sleeping?" They might be speculative, for example, "Mother Hubbard, why did you run out of bones?" or "Boy Blue, why were you sleeping on the job?"

Interviewers often use three types of questions involving a celebrity's past, their experience in the adventure, and their future plans to generate a provocative interview. These questions, of course, are imaginative with no right answer and develop critical thinking. The questions are as follows:

1. How did you happen to get involved in your experience (i.e. of candle leaping, going up a hill for water, or guarding sheep)?

2. What was the most exciting, difficult, or scary part of the adventure? Bo-Peep might describe losing her sheep; the robin in "The North Wind..." his feeling freezing cold; and Jack Horner, discovering the plum.

3. What do you plan to do in the future? Jack be Nimble might describe his next athletic attempt. Humpty Dumpty and Jack and Jill might explain how they will avoid future falls and advise others how to avoid them.

TV Talk Conflict Show

TV Talk Conflict shows feature characters describing a conflict to the studio audience who then advises them how to resolve it. For example, when using "Little Miss Muffet," the host (the teacher or a student) introduces the two guests and describes the conflict. The guests, Miss Muffet and the Spider, explain what happened from their points of view.

Miss Muffet might describe how she was eating and the spider intentionally scared her. The spider might argue that he was only strolling through the garden. The host then asks the two to replay in slow motion the action just before the moment she got scared to let the audience see what went on. Finally, the audience questions the guests and suggests what they might do to resolve future conflicts. And, a student playing a psychologist or other "expert" gives advice.

TV Cooking Show

Everyone enjoys eating. Cooking shows develop language and acting skills.

Participants get so involved in describing the food and in pretending to cook and eat it that self-consciousness disappears.

In a "Mother Goose Cooking Show," Mother Goose characters who are involved in eating become experts on the foods in their rhyme. For example, Jack Horner becomes a "Pie Expert." He shows and tells the audience how to make a Christmas pie (or Thanksgiving, Valentine's, or other variation). The Queen in "Sing a Song of Sixpence," becomes a bread and honey expert describing the type of honey she serves and the kinds of bread that go best with it. She might also discuss other foods that she serves at parties besides "bread and honey" and show how she lays them out on her table.

Miss Muffet describes the ingredients in "curds and whey" and other things to add to them (such as fruit or chocolate) to make them tasty. Mother Hubbard suggests foods to serve a dog if you run out of bones. (Students might research Mother Goose books to find other rhymes with foods and create their own cooking show variations).

DEVELOPING EXPRESSIVE STAGE SPEECH

The voice is a musical instrument. We use our voice to communicate a variety of purposes and intents depending on our motivation. For example, say "good-bye" in a tone communicating you never want to see someone again. Now say "good-bye," to mean you hope to see the person soon.

Mother Goose rhymes with their dramatic language are ideal for experimenting with using the voice to express different meanings. Using "Humpty Dumpty" as an example, have students recite the rhyme communicating it as:

- Newscasters trying to convince audiences that Humpty's fall is a great tragedy.

- Comedians trying to convince an audience that the incident is the world's funniest joke.

- Humpty's parents as a way to caution him and other young people to stop sitting on walls.

- Citizens convincing city councilors to get rid of unsafe walls.

- Judges lecturing Humpty because he was a trespasser who deserved to fall.

Try singing "Humpty Dumpty" in different styles. Sing the rhyme as grand opera, chant-sing it as a rap, sing and dance it as a lively musical comedy number.

After the class experiments reciting "Humpty Dumpty" in different ways, divide students into groups giving each a copy of the "Mother Goose Rhymes to Dramatize and Pantomime" from the Appendix. Groups choose a rhyme and practice dramatizing with two different intents or musical styles. After practicing, the groups present their interpretations to the class who guess what style or intent the group is trying to convey.

DEVELOPING ENGLISH LANGUAGE THROUGH DRAMA

The following techniques help both English learners and native speakers develop language and experience it. The techniques are helpful to English language learners because they are involving and make language real, sensual, and fun. Many of the activities are done in a group, creating what psychologist Fritz Kunkel calls the "We Experience."

GESTURING

Gesturing is a universal language. It is true that "actions speak louder than words." Gestures usually get more attention than words. The best speakers use gestures to involve an audience and to emphasize key points. Gestures, of course, also involve the person making the gesture. The body and psyche become aroused by "doing" the word.

For example, have students say, "Let's unite" while making a big circular "unite" gesture around their head. The gesture helps everyone experience the feeling of uniting more than if they just said, "unite" alone. Say, "Some feel depressed," and bend over and droop in a listless depressed fashion. Everyone will experience the "depressed" feeling.

Mother Goose rhymes with their vivid verbs encourage plentiful gestures. When dramatizing in groups, tell students to make a gesture to dramatize every line in a rhyme. This may seem excessive. However, everyone will enjoy this abundant gesturing if it is done enthusiastically and not frivolously or inexpressively. Students profit from adding gestures whenever they read aloud or speak before the class. It brings life into their reading and their experiencing of it.

CHANTING

Chanting comes from the word enchant. The magical repetition of half singing and half speaking implants the language in the psyche. Children chant when learning new words. For example, a three-year-old learning "rich" marches around singing "rich, rich, rich," swinging their arms with a musical rhythm and beat.

Chanting a rhyme emphasizes its rhythm. Couple the chanting with a gesture to illustrate the word and learning is more complete.

For example, when reciting "Hickory, Dickory, Dock," pause at the end of the line, "The mouse ran up, the clock" and repeat "up, up, up, up the clock."

At the same time, have your voice go up and your fingers run up, up, up, up the side of your leg to illustrate "up." Repeat this for "The mouse ran down, down, down, down" reversing the pitch of your voice and direction of your fingers.

Another method is to pick unknown words and chant them before dramatizing. For example before reciting the rhyme, "Old King Cole," chant "merry, merry, merry, merry" while bobbing your head and body merrily. Before reciting, "Hey, Diddle, Diddle," chant "moon, moon, moon, moon," while making a crescent moon shape with your arms.

ADDING VOCALIZED SOUND EFFECTS
AND EXCLAMATIONS

Everyone enjoys creating vocalized sound effects and verbal exclamations, such as WHIRRRR!, BOOM!, OH, WOW!, and OH, GEE! These vocalizations make literature and language down-to-earth and fun. Students profit from knowing that sound effect and animal sound words are language too. Indeed, nonsense writers consciously use them to add zing to their verse.

Mother Goose rhymes with their strong actions and characters invite the addition of sound effects made with the voice, teeth, tongue, palate, and body.

To encourage students to create sound effects, use them yourself. Say, "YUM, YUM, YUM" enthusiastically when eating delicious foods. Open your eyes and utter a long, deep "MOOOOO" as a contented cow. Bark, "WOOF, WOOF, WOOF," energetically as a dog wanting a bone. Say, "OW, OW, OW!" miserably as Jack and Jill taking a hard fall.

SINGING THE RHYMES

Perhaps more than any other technique, singing loosens up a group and creates an emotional bond. Many Mother Goose rhymes have known tunes. Both "Baa, Baa, Black Sheep" and "Twinkle, Twinkle, Little Star," are often sung to the ABC or Alphabet Song. Others, such as "Humpty Dumpty," can be adapted a bit and sung to this tune. You and the students might also make up a tune that seems to fit. Or, invent a chant in a half-spoken, half-sung voice to a rhyme such as "Hickory, Dickory, Dock."

CHAPTER FOUR

Setting the Scene:
Costume Pieces and Rhythm Instruments

SETTING THE SCENE

Costume pieces and musical instruments capture people's attention. Don a paper hat with bright feathers, hold a triangle high, and tap it three times, and an audience will be captivated. Instruments and costume pieces introduce students to the theatrical elements of costume and sound. They help language learners understand and enjoy the drama. They make the literature memorable.

In Chapter Six, the "Dramatizing a Play" page for each rhyme suggests costumes and rhythm instruments to dramatize each rhyme. The Bibliography at the end of the book provides additional sources of information on creating simple costumes and creating and obtaining instruments.

COSTUMES AND FABRICS

Suggestive costume pieces and fabrics for scenic effects stimulate the imagination. They also loosen inhibitions for the players, giving them permission to become another character. Students often ask, "Where is my costume?" Give them a beanie to become Humpty Dumpty or a black wool cap to be a sheep, and they're ready to assume a role.

It's fun and creative to find or make just the right costume piece. Pieces should be simple to keep the dramatization uncomplicated and to place the emphasis where it should be—the development of the imagination. For example, a puffy flowered shower cap and shawl captures the overly helpful Old Mother Hubbard, and floppy felt ears on a headband portray her anxiously hungry dog. A silver star covered with glitter and suspended from a thin black stick with fish line makes a radiant twinkling star.

Costume pieces can be obtained from your throwaways, thrift stores, garage sales and inexpensive variety or party-supply stores. Costume shops often carry inexpensive animal headpieces and character hats. Stock up at Halloween or at after-Halloween sales.

It is particularly exciting and imaginative to create costumes from recyclable materials. Hats of all types, for example, can be made from grocery bags or paper cups and paper plates fastened under the chin with elastic band or ribbon.

A simple no-fuss way to store them is to put them in boxes marked Men, Women, Animals, Fabrics, and Props.

COLLECTING COSTUME PIECES

The following gives general suggestions for obtaining costume pieces and props.

- Hats of all types in general make the best costume piece. A hat shows the role we want to assume. Crushable felt hats can be adapted for many purposes. Flip up the brim, add a rosette and create a Duke of York's Napoleonic-style hat. Tilt the hat on the head at an angle and add a feather for a debonair man. Encircle it with flowers for Mary, Mary Quite Contrary or one of her pretty maids.

- Baseball caps and visors are most versatile. They make excellent animal or bird headpieces. Wear the bill forward to create a critter with a bill or snout. Ears may be attached. Turn the bill around for snoutless critters. Flip up the brim for spunky boys.

- Shawls are theatrical and move well. They may be used as birds' wings or for maids both old and young. Hold the edge of the shawl and tremble to display old age. Fling it around lightly or tie it around the waist to depict carefree youth. Flutter the shawl up and down for a swirling wind effect.

- Gloves can be used almost as puppets. Wear dark gloves to create a creeping spider or a flying blackbird. Don silver or white gloves to create silver bells, cockle shells, and a twinkling star.

MAKING COSTUMES FROM RECYCLABLE MATERIALS

Using recyclable materials shows students that it is often unnecessary to buy something to create a costume. In fact it is more inventive and better for the environment to make one from found objects.

Using costumes made from such things as paper cups and fast-food containers delights an audience when they see this mundane object used in an unusual way. These off-the-wall costumes are perfectly in keeping with the spirit of Mother Goose rhymes.

An interesting project is to have students collect used containers and see what types of costumes and props they can create from them. The following costumes might be made from recyclable materials.

PAPER CUP COSTUMES: Paper cups of different sizes can be used for a variety of costumes. For example, make a bird's beak from a white or yellow cup placed over the nose and held around the head with elastic band. Paint a cup brown to become a dog's snout. Make a boy's hat from a bright colored cup or a girl's with bows or flowers on it. Cut a hole out of the bottom for Boy Blue's horn.

PAPER PLATE HATS: Paper plates make ingenues hats tied under the chin with pastel colored ribbon. Attach paper flowers or bows on top.

GROCERY BAG HATS: Grocery bags can be adapted to the animal or character desired. Roll up the top of the bag until the opening is the right size to fit on the head. Place it on the head and crush it into the shape and size desired. Paint the bag or leave it plain. Add a feather for a perky page, construction paper ears for a dog, and ribbons, tinsel, and flowers for pretty maids.

USING FABRICS

In these dramatizations, students become the scenery with their bodies. Using lightweight fabrics to create the scenery inspires creative movement. For example, whip black material around to create a howling North wind or kneel and hold up red fabric to create Humpty's wall.

Fabrics should be lightweight and relatively small for easy maneuverability. For the classroom, a suggestion of the atmosphere is enough. For example, two-yards of sheer blue nylon held behind a twinkling star would suffice to create a nighttime sky.

Nylon fabrics are lightweight. Netting comes in a variety of colors, is inexpensive, and can be balled up and stored easily. Netting creates beautiful mystical effects and also can be tied around the waist or shoulders as a costume.

ATMOSPHERE STICKS

The weather can be expressed by dowels with strips of cloth, crepe paper, tinsel, or ribbons attached and moved around dramatically. The sticks add a dance-like quality to the drama. Twist around and bend down while swirling a dowel with strips of white crepe paper for the North wind's snow. Wiggle a dowel with a star suspended by fish line to create a twinkling star.

INCORPORATING MUSICAL INSTRUMENTS

A central quality of Mother Goose rhymes is their music. There is music in the rhythm and rhyme. The words themselves are often musical.

Even the most reluctant students enjoy making sound effects with rhythm or homemade instruments. Both playing rhythm instruments and creating them from found objects develops musical intelligence.

Adding rhythm instruments emphasizes this music. Striking a rhythm instrument at the right time can also emphasize and punctuate the wonderful action in the rhymes. For example, strike a drum firmly on Humpty's "great fall." Shake rattles briskly for sheep "wagging their tails behind them." Tap a triangle lightly to "twinkle" like the star.

To tap or beat out a rhythm, use percussion instruments, such as woodblocks or drums. Choose appropriate ones to fit the characters and actions. For example, tap a woodblock in "Hickory, Dickory, Dock," to simulate the ticking of the clock. Stike a drum in "Oh, the Grand Old Duke of York," to resemble the cadence of the marching men.

Effects should be played crisply and emphatically to communicate to the audience clearly and must capture the quality desired. For example, shaking a tambourine for Miss Muffet's hysterical reaction to the spider sounds better than tapping a woodblock to make that effect.

Let students experiment to see what instuments or combination of instruments they think best express the language and the action. Sometimes several instruments or combinations of instruments work equally as well. For example, scraping a guiro as the spider creeps toward Miss Muffet creates suspense as does the light tapping of a woodblock.

Many rhythm instruments, such as woodblocks, triangles, jingle bells, shakers, and small triangles are inexpensive. It may be worth having a few of these to let several students experiment with them in groups.

A variety of instruments and other music resources are available at reasonable prices from West Music Company, 1208 5th Street, Coralville, Iowa, 52241.

The following instruments may be used to create many effects.
    Tom tom
    Six-inch triangle
    Jingle bells
    Handbell
    Wind chimes
    Tambourine
    Guiro (large wooden, fish-shaped scraper with a striker)
    Rhythm sticks
    Shakers, such as maracas or calabash rattles
    Woodblock with a mallet

Instruments particularly suited for students grade two and below are drum, woodblock, rhythm sticks, tambourines, jingle bells.

USING THE PIANO

Use a piano to create a variety of effects. For example, tinkle high keys to sound like silver bells. Place an arm down on low keys to emphasize Humpty's fall. Tap middle keys to create prancing horsemen. Open the piano and strum the strings inside to make a howling North wind.

CREATING MUSICAL INSTRUMENTS

An interesting assignment is to have students create their own instruments by recycling containers and using things found around the house. This develops musical discrimination as students discover that some coffee mugs, for example, make a pleasant clink when tapped with a spoon and others, an undesirable clunk.

Suggestions for quick and easy homemade instruments are given below. The Bibliography also suggests books on making instruments.

Rattles: Any container with a lid may be filled with hard objects such as popcorn, beans, and pebbles.

Drums: A wastebasket struck with a wooden spoon or the hand; a coffee can. (Bleach and milk bottles can be used as shakers and also turned and struck on the bottom for a drum).

Rhythm sticks: Two dowels cut one foot long.

Gong: Pot lid struck with a metal spoon.

Woodblock: A block of wood or table top tapped with bottom of a pen or handle of a wooden spoon.

Bell: A glass or ceramic coffee cup that rings when struck by a spoon.

Chimes: Several glasses filled with different levels of water and then struck by a spoon.

Triangle: A glass that gives a ping sound when tapped back and forth on the inside with a spoon.

The "Dramatizing a Play" page for each rhyme in this book suggests rhythm instruments to use to create sound effects for that rhyme. The following key shows the logos used.

INSTRUMENT KEY

In Chapter Six, the "Dramatizing a Play" page for each rhyme in this book suggests rhythm instruments to use to create sound effects. The following key shows the logos used.

Maracas

Woodblock and mallet

Tambourine

Drum

Triangle

Cowbell

Jingle bells

Guiro (Fish scraper)

Dramatizing Mother Goose

CHAPTER FIVE

A Model Lesson: Little Miss Muffet

The following material is a model for teaching the dramatization of Mother Goose rhymes. This introductory lesson, "Little Miss Muffet," has been used successfully (with some variations) with mainstream, gifted, and language learners from preschool to grade eight.

The lesson is only a model, of course, and you will want to add or eliminate activities as you see fit. "Little Miss Muffet" was chosen as an example because it is well-known with two memorable characters. It offers opportunities to play imaginative inanimate objects, and its heightened action lends itself to the teaching of stylized movement. Its unusual language (using words such as *tuffet* and *curds* and *whey*) demonstrates how to develop language and poetry appreciation and understanding through drama.

The material in this chapter is detailed but a thorough grounding in the principles and techniques of dramatization gives students the background to do committed effective dramatizations on their own. A brief description of how to dramatize the rhymes is in Chapter Six, "Dramatizing Mother Goose Rhymes."

INTRODUCING THE DRAMATIZATION OF MOTHER GOOSE RHYMES

Materials

- History of Mother Goose and her rhymes from this book (for use with students grades three and above)

- The three pages in this book devoted to "Little Miss Muffet": The Dramatizing a Play Page, the Dramatic Action Picture Page, and the Developing Language and Drama page

- Other Mother Goose rhyme books—see Bibliography

- Dust cap, apron, shawl, granny glasses or other simple, suggestive Mother Goose costume pieces for the teacher to wear (optional)

• Bell or other control device

• Triangle

GETTING INTO DRAMA AND INTRODUCING THE GOAL

Procedure: To make a transition from the everyday world of the classroom to the magical world of theatre, you, as the teacher-director (perhaps dressed as Mother Goose) hold up a triangle and tap it lightly three times to signal that the drama will begin.

Tell students that they will become the characters and objects in Mother Goose rhymes and fly on the wings of their imaginations to dramatize them. Encourage students to chant with you "Fly, fly, fly," while flapping imaginary wings to immediately "get into drama" and experience the techniques they will use in the lesson.

For students grades four and above, discuss the history of Mother Goose and the rhymes. Mention that most of the rhymes were originally told to adults and come from ballads, songs, adult games, riddles, and even plays by Shakespeare. Most are more than 200 years old.

Describe how nurses and nannies heard them and recited them to infants to entertain them. The ones the children enjoyed endured and were put into books. Mention that the rhymes are a part of our American heritage and that *The Dictionary of Cultural Literacy* includes fifteen Mother Goose rhymes that all Americans should know to be considered culturally literate.

Ask students why both adults and children continue to like the rhymes even after 200 years.

Show students pictures of the rhymes from different books mentioning how artists from both the past and present enjoy drawing them. Ask why artists continually want to illustrate the rhymes.

TEACHING THE PRINCIPLES OF GOOD STAGE SPEECH

Procedure: For students grade three and above, explain that they need to follow four speaking principles to dramatize poetry effectively and to make them come alive. (Younger students learn the techniques by your modeling them and by your informal encouragement and reinforcement).

List the principles on a chart or the board.

PROJECTION: Speaking loudly or throwing your voice out so that everyone hears every word.

ARTICULATION: Speaking all letters and syllables distinctly so that everyone understands the precise word spoken.

COLORIZATION: Coloring your speech and adding gestures so that words come fully alive and sound like what they describe.

SLOW THE PACE: Slowing the rate of speech and pace of the action so that everyone enjoys and understands every word and action.

INTRODUCING THE BELL

Procedure: Introduce the use of the bell for control. Show students the bell and tell them that they will stand and speak and act when you ring the bell and stop and sit down when you ring it again. Mention the importance of having good posture to use the voice fully. The following exercises require simultaneously chanting the name of each principle and making a gesture to dramatize it.

DISCUSSING AND PRACTICING PROJECTION

Procedure: Discuss the meaning of projection or throwing your voice out like a ball to the back of a space to be understood. Demonstrate, saying "Projection" and throwing your arm out strongly as if tossing a ball to the back of the room. Ask what happens to an audience if a speaker projects poorly. Model poor projection. Mumble a short sentence. Then ask, "What was wrong with the way I spoke then if I were performing for an audience?"

Tell students that when you ring the bell, they will stand and pretend to throw or project a ball to the front of the room while chanting PROJECTION four times.

REINFORCING PROJECTION

Procedure: Praise those enthusiastically projecting. Mention that the most important quality of a good actor is a strong, expressive voice. Explain that directors of student plays often first look for actors who project well when casting a leading or narrator role in a play. Mention that poor projection is the central problem with many student performances and some adult ones, too.

DISCUSSING AND PRACTICING ARTICULATION

Procedure: Discuss articulation or saying letters and syllables in words distinctly so that the precise word is understood. Mention that British speakers often have excellent diction so that we know exactly what is being said.

Model poor and then good diction. Say "cat," slurring the "t." Say it again emphatically pronouncing the final "t." Ask students, "What did I do differently the second time to make the word clear?"

Tell them to stand on the bell signal and to point emphatically with an index finger to emphasize each syllable while chanting AR TIC U LA TION four times emphasizing each syllable.

REINFORCING GOOD DICTION

Procedure: Praise their distinct articulation. Ask why good articulation is essential in reciting poetry that often uses only a few words. Practice saying other words from the rhymes such as, "Hickory, dickory, dock" or "Oh, the grand old duke of York," using good articulation. (Perhaps use spelling words or words from their readers for further practice).

DISCUSSING AND PRACTICING COLORIZATION

Procedure: Discuss colorization or speaking colorfully so that words sound like what they describe. For example, deepen your voice and make it sound big and full, and the word *huge* sounds huge; or raise the pitch and speak almost falsetto, and the word *teeney* sounds teeney.

On the bell signal, students stand and chant COLORIZATION four times making a big colorful gesture with their arms as they chant it.

REINFORCING COLORFUL SPEECH

Procedure: Praise wholehearted participation. Mention that colorization is the actor's favorite tool to make language and literature come alive. Practice speaking opposite words colorfully such as huge and tiny; joy and gloom; high and low; bold and timid; fiery and icy.

Try color words. For example, say "green" making it sound like beautiful fresh spring green grass. Say "blue" making it sound like a soft blue spring sky. Say "purple" making it sound royal and important. Let students choose words to try.

DISCUSSING AND PRACTICING SLOWING THE PACE

Procedure: Discuss the importance of slowing the pace to help an audience understand and enjoy the literature and language. Recite "Little Miss Muffet" rapidly. Ask what was wrong with your recitation. Mention that slowing the pace is essential when reciting poetry in which every word counts. It is mandatory in the recitation of Mother Goose rhymes that are short and full of action.

On the bell signal, have students stand and slowly open their arms out to their sides while chanting SLOW-THE-PACE four times focusing on a slow rate of speech and slowed down action.

DISCUSSING LITTLE MISS MUFFET TO PREPARE TO ACT IT

Procedure: Show the "Developing Language and Drama" picture of Miss Muffet from Chapter Six. Discuss her clothes and the type of a little girl she is. Discuss what happens to her.

DRAMATIZING LITTLE MISS MUFFET
WITH YOU AND THE STUDENTS ACTING ALL THE PARTS TOGETHER

Procedure: Tell students that on the bell signal, they will stand and recite the rhyme, "Little Miss Muffet," with you practicing the speaking skills of projection, articulation, colorization, and slowing the pace. Mention that you will also do an action to dramatize each line. Demonstrate this.

Explain that in order to make drama artistic and controlled, they will begin each rhyme by making a frozen picture of the character in the middle of their first and last actions. For example, show how they will curtsy and freeze as Miss Muffit to introduce the character.

Ring the bell and assume the curtsy pose, waiting for students to take the position. When all are ready, act the rhyme following the speaking principles and making clear, enlarged gestures. Freeze at the end of the rhyme creating a final "frozen picture" of Miss Muffet with hands thrown up in air and mouth and eyes open wide in fright. Gesture students to sit down saying, "SIT DOWN," emphatically and rhythmically to help them focus on the next task.

REINFORCING EFFECTIVE DRAMATIZATION

Procedure: Point out specifics of good projection, articulation, colorization, and slowing the pace. Since many of the rhymes are active, praise particularly controlled slowed-down gestures and speech. Make a point to compliment those who act and recite wholeheartedly and then sit and focus quickly, ready to act the next rhyme.

Next dramatize three or four other rhymes (of your choice) with you and the students dramatizing together to loosen imaginations and to teach them the procedure before proceeding to the next step which is guiding students to dramatize the rhymes as plays.

DRAMATIZING MISS MUFFET AS A PLAY
(ACTING ACTIVITIES)

Procedure: After you and the students have enacted several rhymes dramatizing all of the parts, older students and language learners in particular profit from enacting the rhymes as plays. Students grades two and below also benefit from this but often want to play all the parts. The teacher of these younger students then should modify this approach—for example, use several Miss or Mr. Muffets who act along with the teacher and at some point give every child an opportunity to try. All students enjoy the following acting activities. They celebrate the play of the imagination and make these universal character types come alive for people of all ages.

DISCUSSING THE THREE PRINCIPLES OF GOOD ACTING

Procedure: For students grades three and above, explain that students need to follow three principles of good acting. For students grades two and below, just mention that they need to make believe, use control, and use their voices and bodies to show what the characters are doing and feeling.

For those able to read, list the three principles on a chart or the chalkboard.

BELIEVING: Believe that you are the part you are playing.

CONTROL: Exercise control over your actions and emotions.

VOICE AND MOVEMENT: Use voice and movement expressively to portray different characters.

General Procedure: As with the four speaking principles, students discuss each principle briefly and then practice it. The following gives all the elements necessary to prepare students to enact the rhyme successfully and artistically as a play and to do successful dramatizations on their own in groups. These exercises are detailed but a careful laying of this groundwork will be most beneficial in helping students learn the requirements of good theatre.

DISCUSSING BELIEVING

For grades three and above, ask what it means to say that actors must believe they are the parts they are playing to make the drama seem real. Use the film, "The Wizard of Oz," as an example of adult actors playing parts in a children's story. Then, do the following "eating a bowl of curds and whey" activity to practice believing.

DISCUSSING CURDS AND WHEY TO PREPARE
TO ACT EATING THEM

Procedure: Show the "Developing Language and Drama" picture of Miss Muffet eating curds and whey from Chapter Six. Ask what curds and whey are. Reinforce guessing, because it encourages figuring out the meaning of words from the context, a skill used in reading. Many assume, for example, that curds and whey is porridge because this is what Goldilocks eats. If no one knows the word's meaning, clarify that it's cottage cheese with the curds, the thick cheese bits and the whey, the milky part. Tell students that years ago, parents put in big red sweet strawberries to make the curds and whey taste delicious.

EATING CURDS AND WHEY

Procedure: To help stimulate the senses and believability, read each of the following suggestions to have students experience eating curds and whey.

- Before you is a big shiny blue bowl with curds and whey and big sweet sugary strawberries and juices in the bottom. Pick up your bowl and show me its size. Put it down before you. Look deep into the bowl. Pick up a big silver spoon and stir up the bottom so the sweet red strawberries and juices blend together.

- Now dip deep down into the bowl and get the biggest strawberry on your spoon. Look carefully at the big, sweet strawberry. Pop it into your mouth. Slowly chew that big berry tasting all those sweet juices. Swallow it. Lick your lips. Ummmmm…delicious!

- Now you are thirsty. Pick up a frosty glass of pink lemonade and take a big drink.

- There's strawberry juice on your lips and mouth. Pick up a white linen napkin, shake it out and dab the juices from around your mouth. Lick your lips.

After dramatizing, reinforce believable acting. Say such things as, "I saw people really examining the big strawberry. I really believed some of you were chewing that sweet berry and swallowing it. You looked as if you had a big starched white napkin when you shook it out."

BECOMING MISS OR MR. MUFFET IN A SCENE USING CONTROL

Procedure: Discuss the need to use control to make the drama artistic and a success. Mention how actors often use stylized movements and that they must stop and start actions on cue.

Depending on space and the age level, several students or the whole class might participate together in this activity. Boys pretend to be Little Mr. Muffet wearing short white pants and shirts and big, pastel-blue bow ties.

SETTING THE SCENE

Procedure: Tell students that on the bell signal, they will pretend to be a four or five year old girl or boy from one hundred years ago wearing their best clothes. Explain that the front of the room is their garden with big red tulips. They will first skip into the garden as Miss or Mr. Muffet. Next, they will pluck three big red tulips for their moms. They will look at the tulips. Lastly, they will skip back to their seats (their homes) and pretend to hand their moms the flowers. Mention that they will need to use good control so that each Little

Miss or Mr. Muffet has her or his own space and doesn't bump into another Miss or Mr. Muffet.

Ring the bell and coach students through this procedure.

Praise those using good control by doing the actions on cue and not bumping into each other.

BECOMING THE SPIDER WITH CONTROL

Procedure: Explain that the part in which the spider springs and frightens Miss Muffet needs control. For older students, explain that actors take classes in stage combat, and that all aggressive actions on the stage and screen are choreographed.

DISCUSSING SPIDERS TO PREPARE TO BECOME ONE

Procedure: Show pictures of the spider from this book and perhaps from science books. Discuss a spider's body parts and the fact that it has eight legs, weaves webs, and creeps sideways

BECOMING SPIDERS

Tell students to perform the following actions when you ring the bell:

- Make your body look spider-like with eight legs, scowl, and hide on the top of your web.

- See Miss Muffet. "Freeze" on your web and look at her.

- First, creep slowly and quietly down your web. Make sure she can't see or hear you. "Freeze."

- Next, creep quietly sideways to Miss Muffet so she can't hear you. Crouch next to her, making sure she can't see you.

- Finally, on a count of three, spring at Miss Muffet, make a spidery sound and "Freeze."

REINFORCING CONTROL

Procedure: Point out specifics of good control such as how some crept slowly and quietly so no one could see or hear them.

BECOMING A TUFFET AND BOWL USING VOICE AND MOVEMENT

Procedure: Discuss how actors use their voices and movements to show who their characters are and what they are doing and feeling. Point out how well students used their voices and movements to portray the spider in the exercise above. Ask why voice and movement are the actor's most important tools.

Explain that they will do another exercise using movement and their imaginations to become the objects in the rhyme.

DISCUSSING TUFFETS TO BECOME ONE

Procedure: Ask them to guess the meaning of tuffet. They will likely guess a cushion, stool, or little hill and perhaps even a toadstool or mushroom as this is how it's been portrayed by different artists. Discuss the fact that tuffet is a made-up word. Ask why the poet used tuffet instead of chair, stool, or another seat for Miss Muffet?

You might mention that nonsense writers often make up playful words. Later, they might discuss other rhymes, such as "Hickory, Dickory, Dock" and "Hey Diddle, Diddle" that use made-up words to create certain sounds.

Mention that since artists depict tuffets as different things, that they may become any kind of tuffet they desire when you ring the bell.

BECOMING TUFFETS

Procedure: Ring the bell, and as students become tuffets, go around and pretend to sit on some tuffets to reinforce their creativity and participation. Comment on their different imaginative shapes and styles and the fact that they have wonderful imaginations.

BECOMING BOWLS OF CURDS AND WHEY

Procedure: Tell students that they will now transform into curds and whey in bowls of any size or shape desired. Ring the bell; and then go around and eat from the various bowls to again reinforce participation and creativity. Comment on the different shapes and sizes; and point out that each has created her or his unique bowl. Some may even depict animated curds and whey wiggling in the bowl. Dip in an imaginary spoon and eat some. Students are now ready to dramatize the story as a play.

DRAMATIZING RHYMES AS PLAYS

Materials: "Dramatizing a Play" page of Little Miss Muffet from Chapter Six
Rhythm Instruments: Jingle bells, drum, maraca, guiro, and tambourine
Costume Pieces: Frilly shower cap for Miss Muffet, black or brown gloves for the spider.
Procedure: Choose students to play each character and object and select others to make sound effects using the "Dramatizing a Play" page script. For students, preschool to grade two, several students play the leading role along with

the teacher. The remainder of the students act along with the actors while sitting or standing.

Determine where to have the classroom "stage" (usually the front of the room) and clarify where the actors will act when their parts come up. For a first run through, explain that you will recite the rhyme, and students will dramatize their parts when they come up. Explain that you will pause at the end of each line to give the actors time to act their parts and the audience time to enjoy the acting.

Review the procedure. For example, say, "When I recite 'Little Miss Muffet,' Miss Muffet will skip to the center of the stage. When I say, 'sat on a tuffet,' the tuffet will form behind her and Miss Muffet will pretend to sit." Mention that actors only act when the rhymes say to do so. Otherwise, there would be so much going on that the audience wouldn't know where to focus.

Discuss and practice the creation of sound effects. For example, ask, "How should the drum be struck when Miss Muffet sits on the tuffet? How might the guiro be scraped when the spider sneaks on?" Explain that sound effects must be made crisply and clearly to communicate to the audience. Let them experiment and help those who need guidance.

Encourage fluent speakers to ad-lib dialogue. For example, ask, "What might Miss Muffet say when she sees the spider? What does the spider say as he scares her? What might the bowl of curds and whey say or the tuffet?"

Cast the play using the "Cast List." Choose a sound crew to create the sound effects. Place the sound crew along one side of the room to let the audience watch them create the effects. Give Miss Muffet and the Spider costume pieces. (Inanimate objects have no costumes for this informal performance.)

For grades three and above, instruct the student audience to watch closely and be ready to critique those who acted their parts believably and which sound crew members created effects that enhanced the action. The audience should also tell what might be added to improve or enhance the playing.

Tell actors to make a "frozen picture" of the characters in their final action at the end of the rhyme to create theatrical artistry. To create focus, ring a little bell and say, "Curtain" to begin and end the playlet.

PREPARING TO DRAMATIZE IN GROUPS

Students usually say their favorite drama activity is creating and performing the rhymes as plays in groups. Understandably, students are highly motivated because they use their ideas and create the drama themselves. Also, they have the pleasure, excitement, and pride of performance. The next activity shows how to guide students to create their own actions to prepare to dramatize on their own in groups.

GUIDING STUDENTS TO CREATE THEIR OWN ACTIONS USING "HICKORY, DICKORY, DOCK"

Materials:
- "Dramatizing a Play" script page of "Hickory, Dickory, Dock" from Chapter Six

- Rhythm Instruments: woodblock

Procedure: Tell students that you will choose volunteers to create the actions for "Hickory, Dickory, Dock."

Choose ten students to come to the front of the room—five will be mice and the other five, their clocks. Then, go through the rhyme line by line asking both the actors and the other students for action suggestions.

For example, ask "What kind of an action might the clocks do to show 'Hickory, dickory, dock?" Try the suggestions. Some might suggest nodding their heads rhythmically as ticking clocks. Others, putting arms around their head in a circle (to create a clock's face) and moving side to side. Others, swinging an arm back and forth as a clock's pendulum. If they have no ideas at first, give some yourself. Then, do the second line asking, "What might the mice do to show, 'The mouse went up the clock.' "

Try each line a variety of ways. Choose one interpretation for each line. Choose a sound crew of one or two students tapping woodblocks for the clock's rhythm and the scurrying mouse. Then, the class as a chorus recites and the five mice and five clocks perform together with the sound crew.

DRAMATIZING RHYMES IN GROUPS

Procedure: Decide whether to have all groups act the same rhyme or to give each group a different rhyme. Make one copy of the "Dramatizing a Play" page for the narrator of each group. Send the groups to various areas in the room to practice their dramatizations.

Let students decide who will play the narrator, character, and objects and who will make sound effects. Or, assign the roles by numbering the parts of the cast list and designating the narrator, for example, as "number one," Little

Miss Muffet as "number two," etc., and then assigning each student a number. Students play the part corresponding to their number on the script.

Give groups about ten minutes to practice. (A brief time focuses creativity and interest). Students then reassemble and present their plays to each other.

After each presentation, have the audience evaluate it. For younger students (grade two and below) focus on congratulating them for using their imaginations and using good control. For older students, ask which actors played their parts believably and what they did specifically with their voices and movements to make the characters come alive. Discuss the sound crew, asking which effects were played crisply and on cue. Finally, ask what might be added next time to enhance the performance.

STUDENT REFLECTION

After dramatizing, students benefit from discussing what they enjoyed doing most and also what they liked most in the rhymes themselves. They also enjoy describing how they felt when they were doing certain actions such as falling, eating, or flying. They might also tell what they found most difficult to do. Students develop a reflective vocabulary as they learn to verbalize their reactions to what may be a moving experience. Reflection provides a welcome and important balance to the active expression of the drama.

Reflection helps teachers see what students enjoy, so that they might emphasize this pleasurable experience again and see what areas need to be worked on. It sometimes gives surprising insights into the reactions of individuals.

A simple effective way to encourage reflection and to integrate drama with art is to have students draw and write about their favorite rhymes. The drawings might be made into a *Mother Goose Rhyme Book* or used as a basis for a mural.

EXTENDING THE DRAMA

Mother Goose rhymes might be dramatized over several days or used throughout the year. A unit might integrate the dramatization with a study of the rhymes as literature and their history. (See Chapters 7, 8, and 9 for background and questions on the poems as works of literature and their history.)

The dramatization might lead to the dramatization of limericks and other nonsense verse and serious poetry. A unit might conclude with a performance for an audience or be part of a family literacy event in which adults and students act together.

CHAPTER SIX

Dramatizing Mother Goose Rhymes

The following three pages on each of the seventeen rhymes give ways to dramatize them.

First, the **"Dramatizing a Play"** page has the rhyme and a written explanation of a dramatic gesture to do with each line. The page has a cast list, suggested rhythm instruments, and costume pieces.

Use the page as a guide for gestures to dramatize the rhymes with everyone in a class acting all of the characters together with you. Also use the page as a guide to stage little plays with individuals cast in separate parts and a sound crew to create sound effects.

This method might be done with the teacher assigning roles to students who perform before the class. Or, students might be divided into groups (with each group getting a copy of this page—their "rhyme script"). Students practice dramatizing in their groups and then perform the dramatization before the class. They might also perform for relatives or other classes.

The **"Dramatic Action Picture"** page has a picture of the characters dramatizing each line of a rhyme with a dramatic gesture and the words of the poem written under the picture. Use the pictures to dramatize the rhyme with the students. Students may also create their own Mother Goose rhyme books to read and act by cutting apart the pictures and stapling them together.

Finally, the **"Developing Drama and Language"** page depicts the rhyme's total action in a picture of one or two scenes. Use the page for discussion and to introduce English language learners and other students to the characters, situation, and total action of the rhyme. After dramatization, use the page as a review to develop language, story sequencing, imagination, and critical thinking.

For more detailed suggestions on dramatization, see Chapter Three, "Techniques to Inspire Dramatization"; Chapter Four, "Setting the Scene"; and Chapter Five, "A Model Lesson: 'Little Miss Muffet.'"

DRAMATIZING
Baa, Baa, Black Sheep

CAST (five or more)
Narrator
Black Sheep
Three Bags of Wool
Master
Dame
Little Boy

COSTUME SUGGESTIONS
Sheep: black cap, perhaps with ears
Master: top hat
Dame: flower in hair or pretty hat
    and shawl
Little Boy: bright knit cap

INSTRUMENT SUGGESTIONS
maracas, triangle, woodblock,
jingle bells

Baa, baa, black sheep,
(Make ears. Speak in sheep's voice.)

Have you any wool?
(Point rhythmically at sheep.)

Yes, sir, yes, sir, three bags full;
(Nod head rhythmically.
Arms make three full bags.)

One for my master,
(Hold up one finger. Make sweeping bow.)

One for my dame,
(Hold up one finger. Curtsy elegantly.)

One for the little boy
Who lives down the lane.
(Hold up one finger. Put thumb over shoulder
pointing down the lane. Then freeze.)

First use the pictures to dramatize the rhyme. Then cut along the dotted lines to form a book.

1

Baa, baa, black sheep,

2

Have you any wool?

3

Yes, sir, yes, sir, three bags full;

4

One for my master,

5

One for my dame,

6

And one for the little boy,
Who lives down the lane.

DRAMATIZING
Hey! Diddle, Diddle

CAST (seven)
Narrator
Cat
Cow
Moon
Little dog
Dish
Spoon

INSTRUMENT SUGGESTIONS
jingle bells, cowbell, tambourine

COSTUME SUGGESTIONS
Cat: cat ears
Cow: black cap with white horns of
 cloth or paper attached
Moon: silver shirt or hold cardboard
 cresecent moon covered with tin foil
Dog: brown baseball cap or brown knit
 cap with floppy cloth ears attached
Dish and Spoon: gray clothing

Hey! diddle, diddle,
(Thrust hands in and out.)

The cat and the fiddle,
(Make cat ears on head and fiddle.)

The cow jumped over the moon;
("Moo," jump, and arms make
crescent moon shape.)

The little dog laughed to see such sport,
(Point with paw and say, "Ha, ha ha!")

And the dish ran away with the spoon.
(Arms make body wide for dish.
Then, make spoon shape over head and run.
Finally, freeze.)

First use the pictures to dramatize the rhyme. Then cut along the dotted lines to form a book.

1

Hey!

2

Diddle, diddle,

3

The cat and the fiddle,

4

The cow jumped over the moon;

5

The little dog laughed to see such sport,

6

And the dish ran away with the spoon.

Dramatizing Mother Goose

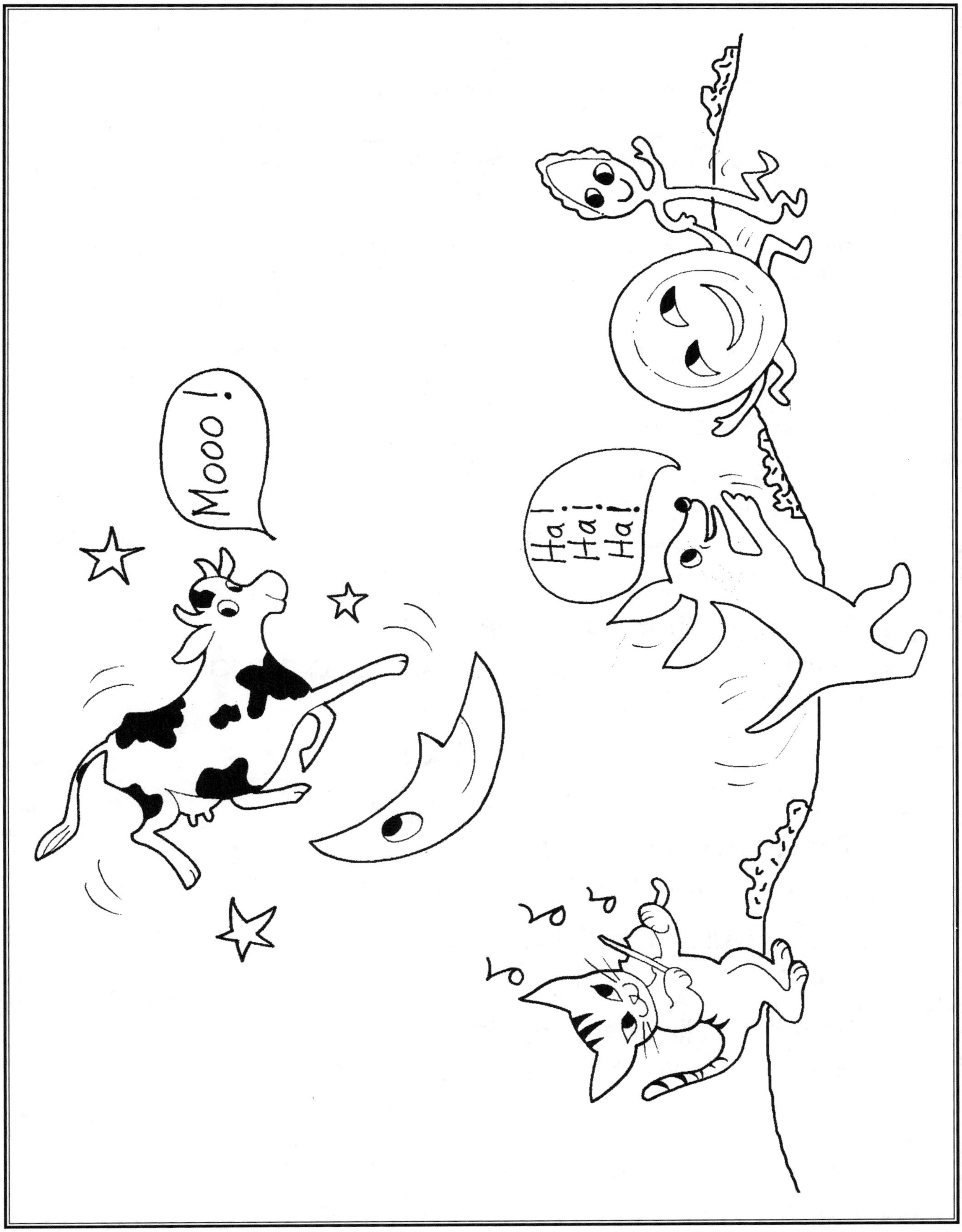
Mooo!
Ha! Ha! Ha!

Hickory, Dickory, Dock

CAST (three or more)
Narrator
Mouse
Clock
(Several students might play mice and clocks)

INSTRUMENT SUGGESTIONS
Tap a woodblock rhythmically to resemble a ticking clock. Tap it briskly as the mouse scurries up and down.

COSTUME SUGGESTIONS
Mouse: paper or felt mouse ears attached to a headband or brown or gray cap
Clock: All black or brown clothes. Or, hold up a cardboard or paper plate clock face and move it by your face rhythmically.

Hickory, dickory, dock,
(Arms make clock's face around head. Move side to side rhythmically.)

The mouse ran up the clock.
(Two fingers run up side of body.)

The clock struck one.
(Thrust out one finger. Say "Bong!")

The mouse ran down.
(Fingers run down.)

Hickory, dickory, dock.
(Repeat first line, and then freeze.)

First use the pictures to dramatize the rhyme. Then cut along the dotted lines to form a book.

1

Hickory, dickory, dock.

2

The mouse ran up the clock.

3

The clock struck one.

4

The mouse ran down.

5

Hickory, dickory, dock.

6

The End!

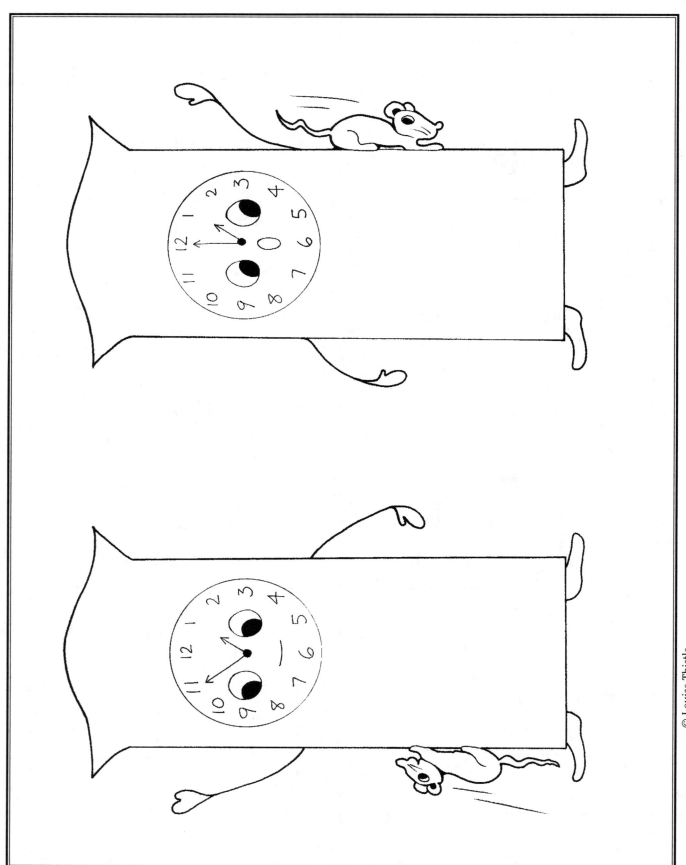

DRAMATIZING
Humpty Dumpty

CAST (five or more)
Narrator
Humpty
Wall (one or more)
King's Horses and Men (two or more)

COSTUME SUGGESTIONS
Humpty: beanie or other funny hat
King's Horses and Men: tall paper soldier hats
Wall: red shirt

INSTRUMENT SUGGESTIONS
drum, woodblock, tambourine

Humpty Dumpty sat on a wall,
(Become a big egg,
wobble, and pretend to sit.)

Humpty Dumpty had a great fall.
(Repeat wobble and fall slowly.)

**All the king's horses and
all the king's men,**
(Prance and whinny or slap knees.)

Couldn't put Humpty together again.
(Shake head, shrug, and then freeze.)

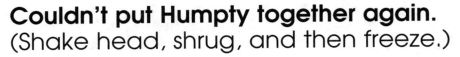

First use the pictures to dramatize the rhyme. Then cut along the dotted lines to form a book.

1 Humpty Dumpty

2 sat on a wall,

3 Humpty Dumpty had a great fall.

4 All the king's horses and all the king's men,

5 Couldn't put Humpty together again!

6 The End!

Dramatizing Mother Goose

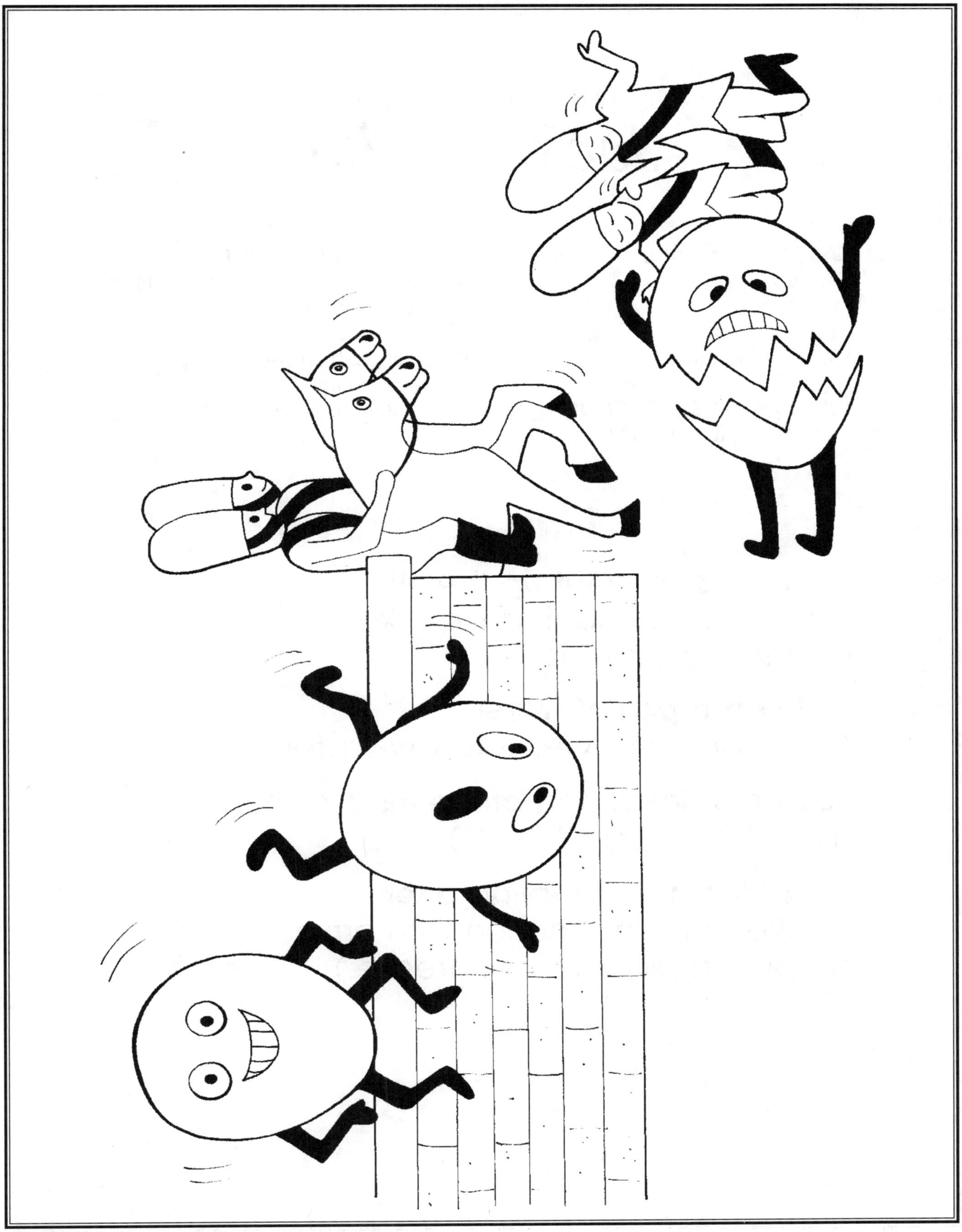

DRAMATIZING
Jack and Jill

CAST (five or more)
Narrator
Jack
Jill
Well (two or more)

INSTRUMENT SUGGESTIONS
jingle bells, guiro, woodblock

COSTUME SUGGESTIONS
Jack: farmer's style hat with wide brim
Jill: hair in braids with ribbons or
    bonnet with long ties
Pail: (optional) one or both together
    may carry plastic bucket
Well: red or gray shirts

Jack and Jill went up the hill
(Hold real or imaginary bucket
and swing arms up.)

To fetch a pail of water,
(Turn handle of well to draw water.)

Jack fell down and broke his crown,
(Hold head. Say, "OW!")

And Jill came tumbling after.
(Make tumbling motion with arms
or spin "in place." Then freeze.)

Dramatizing Mother Goose

First use the pictures to dramatize the rhyme. Then cut along the dotted lines to form a book.

1

Jack and Jill went up a hill

2

To fetch a pail of water;

3

OW!

Jack fell down and
broke his crown,

4

And Jill came tumbling after.

Dramatizing Mother Goose

© Louise Thistle

DRAMATIZING
Jack Be Nimble

CAST (two or more)
Jack
Candlestick.
(Several students might play Jack and the candlestick at the same time)

INSTRUMENT SUGGESTIONS
jingles bells, woodblock

COSTUME SUGGESTIONS
Jack: night cap with tassel or bright knit cap
Candlestick: kneel holding a paper towel or toilet roll candle with orange or red cellophane flame

Jack be nimble,
(Spin around.)

Jack be quick,
(Run "in place.")

Jack jump over
(Jump.)

The candlestick.
(Point at stick or become a
candle and melt slowly.)

First use the pictures to dramatize the rhyme. Then cut along the dotted lines to form a book.

1

Jack be nimble,

2

Jack be quick,

3

Jack jump over

4

The End!

The candlestick.

© Louise Thistle

Dramatizing Mother Goose

Dramatizing Mother Goose

DRAMATIZING
Little Bo-Peep

CAST (four or more)
Narrator
Bo-Peep
Sheep (two or more)

INSTRUMENT SUGGESTIONS
triangle, maracas, woodblock,
jingle bells

COSTUME SUGGESTIONS
Bo-Peep: big bow attached to a headband and perhaps a crook with a
   bow attached
Sheep: white caps with black ears
   attached or white fur material fastened under neck with elastic band,
   fluffy tails pinned in back

Little Bo-Peep
(Curtsy.)

Has lost her sheep,
(Shade eyes and look around.)

And doesn't know where to find them;
(Toss hands up rhythmically.)

Leave them alone,
(Push hands away from body.)

And they'll come home,
(Pull hands toward self.)

Wagging their tails behind them.
(Turn and wag tail. Say, "Baaaa,"
and then freeze.)

First use the pictures to dramatize the rhyme. Then cut along the dotted lines to form a book.

1

Little Bo-Peep

2

Has lost her sheep,

3

And doesn't know where to find them;

4

Leave them alone,

5

And they'll come home,

6

Baa!
Baa!
Baa!
Baa!

Wagging their tales behind them.

DRAMATIZING
Little Boy Blue

CAST (five or more)
Narrator
Boy Blue
Person awakening Boy Blue
Sheep (one or more)
Cow (one or more)

INSTRUMENT SUGGESTIONS
jingle bells, cowbell, tambourine

COSTUME SUGGESTIONS
Person Awakening Little Boy Blue:
  farmer's hat
Boy Blue: bright blue cap, baseball cap
  or construction paper blue hat
Horn: paper towel roll or yellow con-
  struction paper rolled in horn shape
Cow: black or black and white knit cap
  with horns attached
Sheep: white fur caps
Haystack: hold yellow cloth or grains
  of wheat

Little Boy Blue,
(Bow.)

Come blow your horn,
(Tilt horn up. Say, "Toot, toot.")

The sheep's in the meadow,
(Shake head. Say, "Baaaa!")

The cow's in the corn;
(Push head forward. Open
eyes wide. Say "Mooo!")

But where is the boy who
looks after the sheep?
(Shrug and look around.)

He's under a haystack fast asleep.
(Sleep.)

First use the pictures to dramatize the rhyme. Then cut along the dotted lines to form a book.

1

Little Boy Blue,

2

Come blow your horn,

3

The sheep's in the meadow,

4

The cow's in the corn;

5

But where is the little boy
who looks after the sheep?

6

He's under a haystack
fast asleep.

Dramatizing Mother Goose

Dramatizing Mother Goose

DRAMATIZING
Little Jack Horner

Cast (four or more)
Narrator
Jack Horner
Corner (one or two)
Pie (one or two)

INSTRUMENT SUGGESTIONS
jingle bells, maracas, woodblock,
triangle

COSTUME SUGGESTIONS
Jack Horner: green Peter Pan style hat
   (perhaps with a red feather)
Corner: black or brown clothes
Pie: light yellow or other crust color
   shirt

Little Jack Horner
(Bow.)

Sat in a corner,
(Turn and sit.)

Eating his Christmas pie;
(Make big eating and chewing motions.)

He put in his thumb,
(Push thumb deep.)

And pulled out a plum,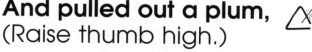
(Raise thumb high.)

And said, "What a good boy am I!"
(Hold out suspenders and
tilt chin up. Then freeze.)

First use the pictures to dramatize the rhyme. Then cut along the dotted lines to form a book.

1

Little Jack Horner

2

Sat in a corner,

3

Yum! Yum!

Eating his Christmas pie;

4

He put in his thumb,

5

And pulled out a plum,

6

And said,
"What a good boy am I!"

Dramatizing Mother Goose

Dramatizing Mother Goose

DRAMATIZING
Little Miss Muffet

CAST (five or more)
Narrator
Little Miss Muffet
Tuffet (one or two)
Bowl of Curds and Whey (one or two)
Spider (one or two)

INSTRUMENT SUGGESTIONS
jingle bells, drum, maraca, tambourine, guiro

COSTUME SUGGESTIONS
Muffet: pink shower or frilly cap
Tuffet: black clothes
Curds and Whey: white clothes
Spider: black or brown garden gloves

Little Miss Muffet
(Curtsy.)

Sat on a tuffet,
(Wiggle to sit.)

Eating her curds and whey;
(Make big scooping motions.)

Along came a spider,
(Walk jaggedly.)

Who sat down beside her,
(Stoop slowly.)

And frightened Miss Muffet away.
(Throw up arms, run "in place.")

First use the pictures to dramatize the rhyme. Then cut along the dotted lines to form a book.

1

Little Miss Muffet

2

Sat on a tuffet,

3

Eating her curds and whey.

4

Along came a spider,

5

Who sat down beside her

6

And frightened
Miss Muffet away.

© Louise Thistle

Dramatizing Mother Goose

DRAMATIZING
Mary, Mary, Quite Contrary

CAST (Eight or more)
Narrator
Mary
Silver bells (2 or more)
Cockle shells (2 or more)
Maids (2 or more)

INSTRUMENT SUGGESTIONS
tambourine, maracas, jingle bells

COSTUME SUGGESTIONS
Mary: hat with flowers and perhaps
 big pink sash and watering can
Silver Bells: ring little bells
Cockle shells: hold up real shells or
 wear white or gray gloves
Pretty Maid: ribbons entwined in hair
 or bows on head of different colors

Mary, Mary, quite contrary,
(Put hands on hips and
sway side to side.)

How does your garden grow?
(Shrug rhythmically. Then water
garden saying, "Sh, sh, sh!")

With silver bells, and cockle shells,
(Hands ring imaginary or real bells. Say,
"Ting-a-ling." Then hands become shells.)

And pretty maids all in a row.
(Hold out edges of skirt and spin.
Then freeze with hands held up
like a ballerina.)

First use the pictures to dramatize the rhyme. Then cut along the dotted lines to form a book.

1

Mary, Mary, quite contrary,

2

How does your garden grow?

3

With silver bells
and cockle shells,

4

And pretty maids
all in a row.

© Louise Thistle

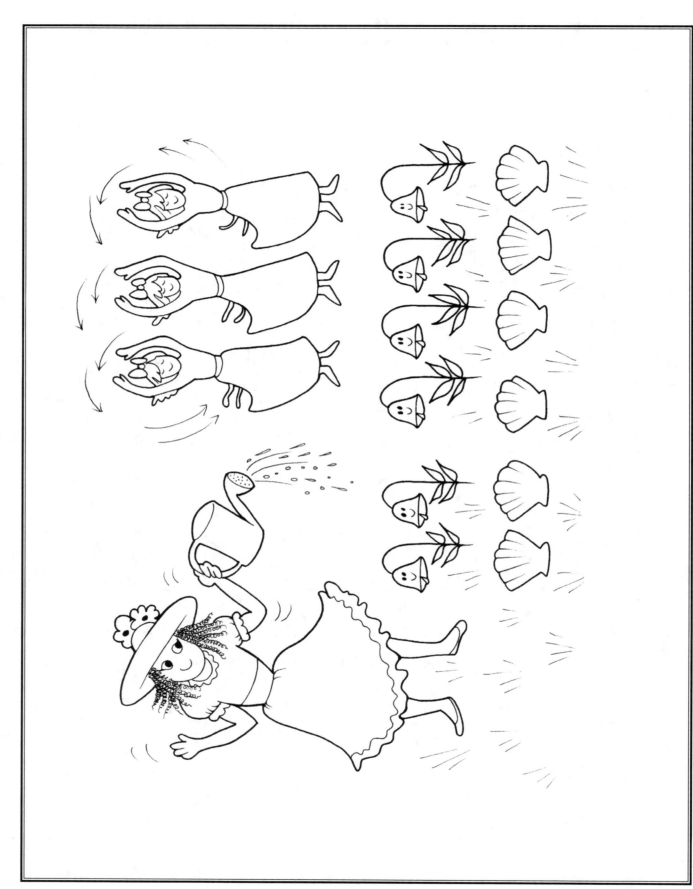

DRAMATIZING
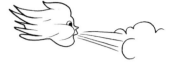
The North Wind Doth Blow

CAST (six or more)
Narrator
North Wind (one or more)
Snow (one or more)
Robin
Barn (two or more)

INSTRUMENT SUGGESTIONS
rattle, triangle, woodblock

COSTUME SUGGESTIONS
North Wind: dark cloth whipped
   around to show howling wind
Snow: white crepe paper attached to a
   stick and fluttered up and down
Robin: brown baseball cap
Barn: black or dark colored clothes

The north wind doth blow,
(Wave arms and say, "SHHHHHHHH!")

And we shall have snow,
(Fingers make falling snow.)

And what will poor robin do then?
The poor thing!
(Shrug and shake head rhythmically.)

He'll sit in a barn,
(Make roof shape with hands.)

And to keep himself warm,
(Hug self.)

He'll hide his head under his wing.
The poor thing!
(Tuck head under wing.
Shake head sadly, then freeze.)

First use the pictures to dramatize the rhyme. Then cut along the dotted lines to form a book.

1

Shhhhh!

The north wind doth blow,

2

And we shall have snow,

3

Boo Hoo!

And what will poor robin do?
The poor thing!

4

He'll sit in a barn,

5

Brrrr!

And to keep himself warm,

6

He'll hide his head under his
wing. The poor thing!

70

Dramatizing Mother Goose

© Louise Thistle

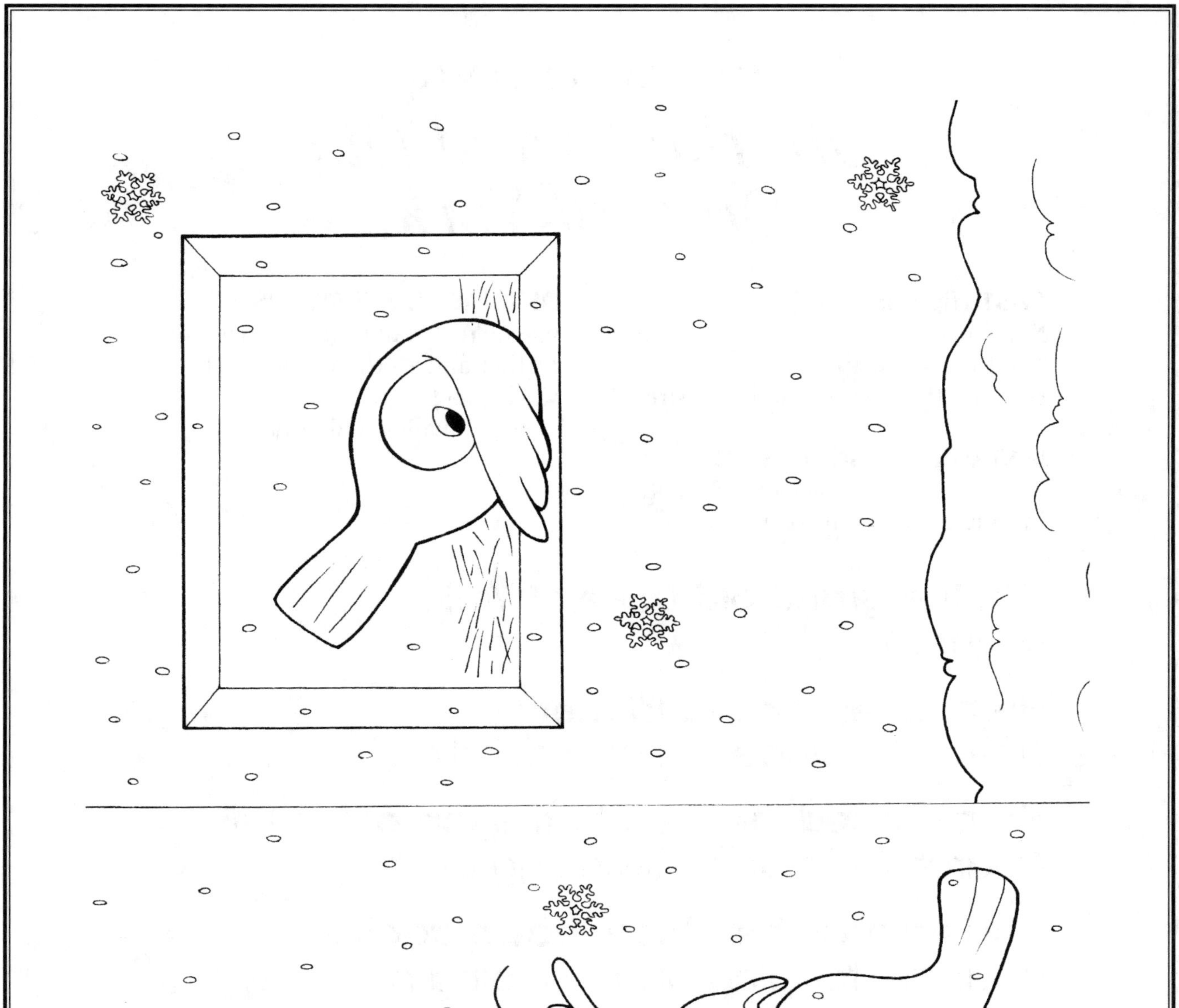

DRAMATIZING
Oh, the Grand Old Duke of York

CAST (five or more)
Narrator
The Duke of York
His Men (four or as many as desired)

COSTUME SUGGESTIONS
Duke of York: tall General's hat with
    feather and a sash across chest,
    wave a flag
His Men: smaller soldier hats

INSTRUMENT SUGGESTIONS
Strike a drum or a woodblock rhythmically throughout the rhyme.

Oh, the grand old Duke of York,
(Salute.)

He had ten thousand men;
(Thrust ten fingers in and out rhythmically.)

He marched them up to the top of the hill,
(March "in place," swinging arms up.)

And he marched them down again.
(March, stooping and swinging arms low.)

And when they were up, they were up,
(Raise arms up.)

And when they were down, they were down,
(Stoop.)

And when they were only halfway up,
(Rise halfway up.)

They were neither up nor down.
(Raise arms up and then stoop down.)

Dramatizing Mother Goose

First use the pictures to dramatize the rhyme. Then cut along the dotted lines to form a book.

1

Oh, the grand old Duke of York,

2

He had ten thousand men;

3

He marched them up
to the top of the hill,

4

And he marched them
back down again.

5

And when they were up,
they were up,

6

And when they were down,
they were down,

7

And when they were only
halfway up,

8

They were neither up
nor down.

DRAMATIZING
Old King Cole

CAST (seven or more)
Narrator
King Cole
Servant with pipe
Servant with bowl
Three fiddlers
Pipe and Bowl: (optional) actors might
  play the pipe and the bowl

INSTRUMENT SUGGESTIONS
jingle bells, woodblock

COSTUME SUGGESTIONS
King Cole: gold or yellow paper
  crown
Servants with pipe and bowl: knit
  caps, each of a different bright color
Three Fiddlers: red berets or berets
  all of the same bright color

Old King Cole was a merry old soul,
(Make belly with arms and bounce rhythmically.)

And a merry old soul was he;
(Keep bouncing. On "merry," grin widely,
holding out corners of mouth with fingers.)

He called for his pipe,
(Beckon and smoke a bubble pipe.)

And he called for his bowl,
(Beckon and stir in bowl.)

And he called for his fiddlers three.
(Beckon, fiddle, and hold up three fingers.)

Tweedle dee, tweedle dee, tweedle dee,
tweedle dee went the fiddlers three.
(Fiddle rhythmically to the words.
Bow and then freeze.)

© Louise Thistle

First use the pictures to dramatize the rhyme. Then cut along the dotted lines to form a book.

1 Old King Cole was a merry old soul,

2 And a merry old soul was he;

3 He called for his pipe,

4 And he called for his bowl,

5 And he called for his fiddlers three,

6 Tweedle dee, tweedle dee, tweedle dee, Tweedle dee went the fiddlers three.

© Louise Thistle

Dramatizing Mother Goose

Dramatizing Mother Goose

DRAMATIZING
Old Mother Hubbard

CAST (four or five)
Narrator
Old Mother Hubbard
Cupboard (one or two)
Dog

INSTRUMENT SUGGESTIONS
rattle, woodblock, triangle

COSTUME SUGGESTIONS
Old Mother Hubbard: frilly cap,
  granny glasses, and a shawl
Cupboard: brown or black clothes
Dog: floppy ears on a headband

Old Mother Hubbard
(Bend over and shake while
holding imaginary cane.)

Went to the cupboard,
(Hobble "in place.")

To fetch her poor dog a bone.
(Paws by chin. Say, "Woof, woof!")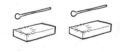

But when she got there,
(Hobble and stop.)

The cupboard was bare,
(Open cupboard. Shake head. Say, "Oh,
dear!")

And so the poor dog had none.
(Paws by face. Tilt head sadly.
Say, "Oh, No!")

First use the pictures to dramatize the rhyme. Then cut along the dotted lines to form a book.

1 Old Mother Hubbard	**2** Went to the cupboard,
3 Woof! Woof! To fetch her poor dog a bone.	**4** But when she got there,
5 The cupboard was bare,	**6** Oh No! And so the poor dog had none.

Dramatizing Mother Goose

DRAMATIZING
Sing a Song of Sixpence

CAST (nine or more)
Narrator
Singer
Blackbirds (2 or more)
Pie
Servant who cuts and serves pie
King
Queen
Maid

INSTRUMENT SUGGESTIONS
jingle bells, rattles, woodblock,
triangle

COSTUME SUGGESTIONS
Singer: lacy material tied around neck
   as lace ruff or peaked hat
Blackbirds: black baseball caps or
   paper cups attached to elastic bands
   and put around head to create beaks
Servant who cuts and serves pie: beret
   or peaked hat
King: crown
Queen: different crown than the king's
   or some fancy headpiece
Maid: white maid's cap

Sing a song of sixpence,
(Cup hands to mouth.)

A pocket full of rye;
(Reach in your pocket and show rye.)

Four and twenty blackbirds,
(Show four fingers and then,
ten fingers, twice. Flap wings.)

Baked in a pie.
(Make pie shape with arms.)

When the pie was opened,
(Cut pie.)

The birds began to sing;
(Flap wings and say, "Tweet, tweet!")

Wasn't that a dainty dish,
(Hold out pie.)

To set before the King?
(Make crown shape on head.)

The King was in his counting-house,
(Stand pompously.)

Counting out his money;
(Count and stack money.)

The Queen was in the parlor,
(Nose in air.)

Eating bread and honey.
(Eat, lick lips.)

The maid was in the garden,
(Skip.)

Hanging out the clothes,
(Reach down and hang out clothes.)

When along came a blackbird,
(Flap wings.)

Who pecked off her nose.
(Grab nose.)

But then came a jenny wren,
(Tweet and flap.)

Who popped it on again.
(Open hands out showing off nose.)

First use the pictures to dramatize the rhyme. Then cut along the dotted lines to form a book.

1

Sing a song of sixpence,

2

A pocket full of rye,

3

Four and twenty blackbirds,

4

Baked in a pie.

5

When the pie was opened,

6

The birds began to sing;

First use the pictures to dramatize the rhyme. Then cut along the dotted lines to form a book.

7

Wasn't that a dainty dish,
To set before the King?

8

The King was in his counting-
house, Counting out his money;

9

The Queen was in the parlor,
Eating bread and honey.

10

The maid was in the garden,
Hanging out the clothes,

11

When along came
a blackbird,
Who pecked off her nose.

12

But then came a jenny wren,
Who popped it on again.

Dramatizing Mother Goose

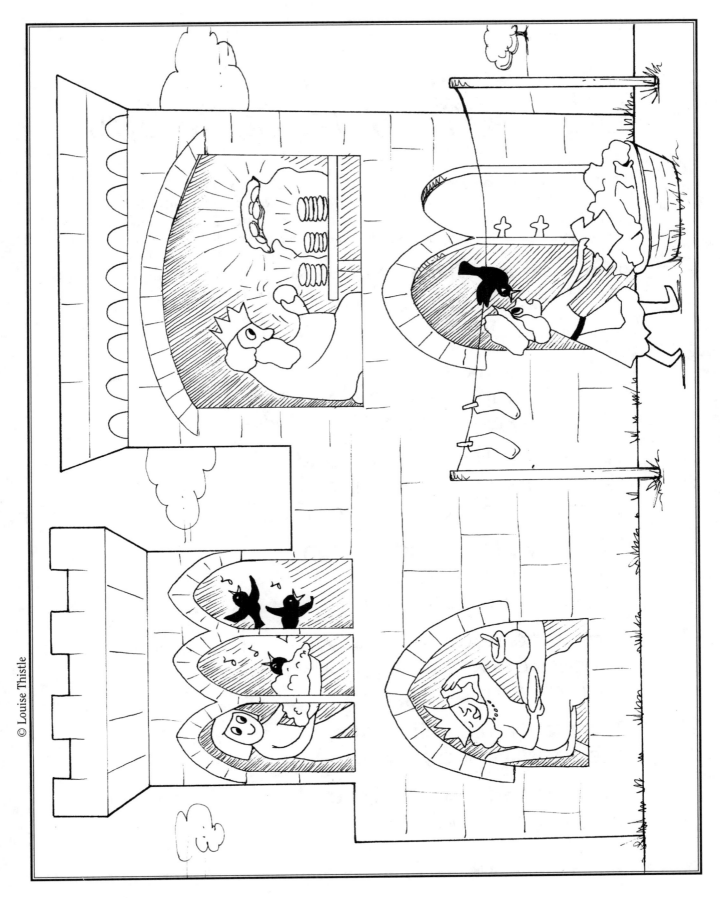

Dramatizing Mother Goose

DRAMATIZING
Twinkle, Twinkle, Little Star

CAST (three or more)
Narrator
Star
Wonderers (one or as many as desired)

INSTRUMENT SUGGESTIONS
jingle bells, triangle

COSTUME SUGGESTIONS
Little Star: Wear a glove with silver sequins or glitter attached to it. Or, attach a silver cardboard star covered with glitter to invisible fish line. Suspend it to a dowel to create a twinkling effect.

Twinkle, twinkle, little star,
(Raise a hand up and open and close it to become a "twinkling star.")

How I wonder what you are!
(Put finger on chin and move head rhythmically "wondering.")

Up above the world so high,
(Arms make circle around head to show the round world.)

Like a diamond in the sky.
(Fingers of two hands make diamond shape.)

Twinkle, twinkle, little star,
(Repeat first line.)

How I wonder what you are!
(Repeat second line.)

First use the pictures to dramatize the rhyme. Then cut along the dotted lines to form a book.

1

Twinkle, twinkle, little star,

2

How I wonder what you are!

3

Up above the world so high,

4

Like a diamond in the sky.

5

Twinkle, twinkle, little star,

6

How I wonder what you are!

CHAPTER SEVEN

The History of Mother Goose Rhymes

Mother Goose is the first literary person most American children encounter. But attempts to trace Mother Goose to any real person have led to many scholarly goose chases. The name likely stems from the old peasant woman who tended the village geese, and also developed the imaginations of the village children by telling them stories.

Later, "Mother Goose" came to represent the many aunts, nannies, nurses, and other women (often single and elderly) who minded children and soothed and amused them with stories, poems and songs.

The first use of "Mother Goose" in connection with nursery rhymes was by English publisher John Newbery. Newbery, the first publisher to produce a line of books just for children, issued *Mother Goose's Melodies: or, Sonnets for the Cradle* probably in 1765 or 1766.

The book had fifty-one rhymes and sixteen lullabies from Shakespeare, and was later pirated (against copyright laws) and published in America. It was one of the first books specifically for children published in this country. A subsequent version was illustrated by artists' drawings in place of the rough woodcuts traditionally used. The popularity of the pictures in this book is credited with making Mother Goose a well-known term in America.

But even though the collected Mother Goose rhymes were first published as a children's book, most of the rhymes were composed to entertain adults. Only the ABC and counting games and lullabies were originally meant for children.

Most of the rhymes are over 200 years old; more than one quarter of them were known in Shakespeare's day. Few were written down, however, before the 19th century. So the rhymes prospered and survived through the oral tradition. Their imaginative characters and situations have inspired artists for over 200 years.

Such famous artists as Randolph Caldecott, Walter Crane, Leslie Brooke, Arthur Rackham and Kate Greenaway in the 19th and early 20th centuries and Tomie de Paola, Arnold Lobel, Brian Wildsmith and James Marshall from contemporary times have illustrated books with the rhymes. For work of contemporary and 18th and 19th artists, see the Bibliography. Indeed, an examination of the illustrations of Mother Goose rhymes over time is a study in the history of children's book illustration.

The rhymes come from diverse sources. Some are stanzas from ballads and folk songs; others are remnants of ancient rituals and old games. Many are bits of dialogue from plays. A few are political satires and adult riddles. Several had a number of verses and were sold on the street in little books costing a few pennies. Some were performed on the London stage in comic plays.

Interest in Mother Goose rhymes is alive today. The Mother Goose Guild Newsletter (listed in the Bibliography) describes events, books and resource materials involving Mother Goose. Eighty-five of its subscribers (both women and men) dress up regularly and appear at libraries, schools, nursing homes and community centers nationwide as Mother Goose.

And in 1987, Gloria Delamar, author of, *Mother Goose From Nursery to Literature,* (listed in the Bibliography) was instrumental in getting Mother Goose day established as May first on Chase's Calender of Events. It is a growing national celebration in which Mother Goose lovers gather to celebrate the rhymes in dramatizations, song, puppet shows, and banquets of cakes, tea and curds and whey. One year, San Francisco held a Mother Goose Parade to honor her, and many radio stations broadcast Mother Goose Day programs on her special day.

The following information is predominantly from *The Oxford Dictionary of Nursery Rhymes* by Iona and Peter Opie. The Opies, who spent ten years researching the history of the rhymes, are considered the foremost authorities on the origin and history of nursery rhymes. For more information on these and other rhymes, see their book and Gloria Delamar's listed in the Bibliography.

BAA, BAA, BLACK SHEEP was recited as early as 1275 as a protest against the export tax on wool. The master is supposedly the king who imposed the tax (receiving the equivalent of a bag of wool); the dame represents the nobility, who got another bag's equivalent; and the little boy, the people, who received only one bag for their labor. It is the framework for Rudyard Kipling's 1888 story, *Baa, Baa, Black Sheep.*

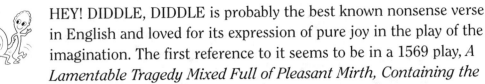

HEY! DIDDLE, DIDDLE is probably the best known nonsense verse in English and loved for its expression of pure joy in the play of the imagination. The first reference to it seems to be in a 1569 play, *A Lamentable Tragedy Mixed Full of Pleasant Mirth, Containing the Life of Cambises, King of Persia* by Thomas Preston: "They be at hand Sir with stick and fiddle; They can play a new dance called hey-diddle-diddle."

HICKORY, DICKORY, DOCK was originally a counting game. To tell time, Westmoreland shepherds called eight, nine, and ten o'clock Hevera (eight), Devera (nne), and Dick (ten). In 1821, a writer in Blackwood's Magazine of Edinburgh, Scotland wrote that the rhyme was being used "by children then and as long as he could remember to decide who was to begin a game." Writer Walter Scott in 1810 recited the rhyme to a young visitor with the words, "Ziccoty, diccoty, dock..."

HUMPTY DUMPTY, according to some scholars, is so old that "its date cannot be measured at all." It is probably the most known rhyme in the English language. Each year probably hundreds of references are made to it in pictures, newspaper and magazine articles and even such commercial items as snack foods.

The rhyme was originally an adult riddle that asked the question, "Who is Humpty that he cannot be put back together again?" (The answer, of course, is an egg.)

The rhyme is known throughout Europe. It's called "Boule Boule" in France; "Hillerin-Lillerin" in Finland and "Humpelken-Pumpleken" in parts of Germany. The figure of Humpty has captured the imagination of writers and cartoonists throughout the ages. Lewis Carroll has devoted a whole chapter to him in *Through the Looking Glass.* In their charming nonsensical conversation, Humpty tells Alice that he can explain to her the meaning of all poems "that ever were invented—-and a good many that haven't been invented just yet."

In the 1995 story, "Who Killed Humpty Dumpty?" by Mickey Zucker Reichert, Humpty exclaims "I was a victim of a terrible yolk."

JACK AND JILL may represent an ancient ceremony. For, as one scholar notes, wells aren't usually located on the tops of hills. Thus, he contends, people in fairy tales would only go to the top of a hill for water if that water had special magical or spiritual significance.

Another scholar believes the rhyme concerns two Scandinavian children, Hjuki and Bill, who were captured by the moon while drawing water. According to this myth, when the moon is full we can see the children holding a pole with the bucket between them.

In the early 1800s, the rhyme with 15 verses was sold on the street in chapbooks (or little books distributed by pedlars or "Chapmen"). Many rhyme books still have all of these verses that tell the further problems Jack and Jill had after their fall on the hill. In the seventeenth century, the names Jack and Jill were used to mean lad and lass.

 JACK BE NIMBLE represents the sport of candle-leaping. Candle leaping was also a fortune-telling game played in England for several centuries. For example, in Wendover, England, the Lace Makers celebrated the St. Catherine Day festivities on Nov. 25th by jumping over a lit candle. If the candle remained lit, the jumper had good luck the following year. St. Catherine's Day was also a popular wedding day in Medieval days.

 LITTLE BO-PEEP was first printed in 1811, but as early as 1364, there was a baby game called "Bo-Peep" similar to our "Peek a Boo." In Shakespeare's time, the adult court played a game called "boe-pepe." Also, there was a popular satirical ballad with the lines "Halfe England ys nought but shepe, In every corner they play boe-pepe."

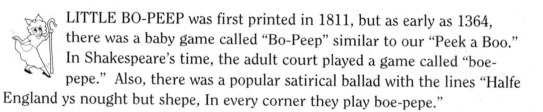 LITTLE BOY BLUE is probably referred to in Shakespeare's *King Lear* when the good Edgar, disguised as Mad Tom, cries to King Lear: "Sleepest or wakest thou, jolly shepherd? Thy sheepe be in the corn. And for one blast of thy minikin mouth. Thy sheep shall have no harm." The character of Boy Blue is also in A. A. Milne's *When We Were Very Young,* but Eugene Field's poem, *Little Boy Blue,* is not connected to the rhyme. The Broadway musical *Come Blow Your Horn* is, of course, taken from the rhyme.

 LITTLE JACK HORNER is supposedly about a Tom Horner who was a servant to an abbot in 1543. The abbot is said to have sent Horner to King Henry VIII with a gift of a pie with the deeds to twelve manors hidden inside. On the way, Horner supposedly "stuck in his thumb and pulled out…" the best property, Mells Manor, for himself. The Horner family denies this, but a Thomas Horner did live in Mells Manor and strange things used to be concealed in pies. See *Sing a Song of Sixpence,* for example.

LITTLE MISS MUFFET is said by some to be Patience Muffet, the daughter of Dr. Thomas Muffet, an entomologist (or bug expert), who wrote a book of verse, *The Silkwormes and Their Flies* in the late 1500s. This is uncertain, however, because the first written version of the verse was in 1805, two hundred years after Dr. Muffet's death.

Some contend the rhyme is more ancient and depicts the "Cushion Dance," a marriage or mating ritual in which a person sits and waits for something important (such as marriage or courtship) to happen.

Miss Muffet is the most frequently illustrated Mother Goose rhyme. A famous portrait is by the French painter, Millais.

MARY MARY QUITE CONTRARY may depict a religious convent with "the silver bells" being the holy bells; the cockleshells, the pilgrim's badges; and the maids in a row, the nuns. Another interpretation is that Mary is Mary Queen of Scots, who liked the carefree life, which angered the stern religious leader, John Knox. In this case, the maids would be her ladies-in-waiting. The phrase, "How does your garden grow?" is frequently used in contemporary gardening articles.

 THE NORTH WIND DOTH BLOW was first printed in 1805 and was set to music in five verses in 1863. It treats a frequent subject of 19th century English verse—the suffering of little birds in the winter. A similar verse of the time says: "Little cock robin peep'd out of his cabin, To see the cold winter come in, Tit, for tat, what matter for that, He'll hide his head under his wing."

OH, THE GRAND OLD DUKE OF YORK has often been thought of as a pompous leader who ordered his solders to do meaningless things such as marching them up and down hills for his own amusement. However, scholars Iona and Peter Opie fail to find historic evidence of this and say that the real Duke of York was a popular and likable chief.

 OLD KING COLE is a popular rhyme with its buoyant expression of enjoying the good life. Attempts to trace King Cole to a real king began when the rhyme was first quoted in a 1708 philosophy book, *Useful Transactions in Philosophy*.

Some try to link him to a King Cole who lived in the third century. The most likely explanation is that he was a rich 16th century merchant named Old Cole who had many servants. In the 1932 poem *King Cole*, poet John Masefield presents the king as a merry old man who plays the flute and is followed by birds, beasts, and butterflies.

OLD MOTHER HUBBARD first appeared in 1805 in a book of eleven verses, *The Comic Adventures of Old Mother Hubbard and Her Dog*. Many rhyme books still have all of these verses that describe the old lady going off on a series of errands for the dog and returning to find him engaged in various pranks.

It probably was written and illustrated by Sarah Catherine Martin. According to legend, Martin wrote the verses after her brother-in-law told her to stop bothering him and to go off and "write one of your stupid little rhymes." The little rhyme was an instant success. One reason for its success is that many believed it was a political satire. The name, "Mother," was a common title in the 16th century for old women of the lower classes. This book began a period in children's literature called by one writer, "The dawn of levity." A clever modern take-off of the rhyme is Dennis Lee's, "The Old Lady and Her Cat," that tells of an old lady sending her cat off on a series of errands which he fulfills in a variety of eccentric hillarious ways.

SING A SONG OF SIXPENCE likely refers to a recipe for a pie in an Italian cookbook. The 1549 recipe describes how "to make pies so that the birds may be alive in them and fly out when it is cut up."

Although this recipe seems unlikely, strange things were often concealed in pies at that time—take for example, the deeds to Horner's pie. Another indication that the rhyme dates to the 16th century is the practice of using "a pocketful of rye" as a measurement of that grain. The rhyme may be referred to in Shakespeare's *Twelfth Night*—"Come on, there's a sixpence for you; let's have a song."

Eve Merriman's poem *Sing a Song of Subways,* follows the words of the poem closely in a modern clever take-off of people packed in a subway and then bursting out. The phrase "Sing a Song of..." is frequently used in titles of books and magazine articles.

 TWINKLE TWINKLE LITTLE STAR BY Jane Taylor first appeared in 1806 in *Rhymes for the Nursery* written with her sister, Ann. The two are considered the first English authors to write exclusively for children and, unlike most poets, actually made money from their poems.

The poem is often printed because of its lyrical beauty and lulling quality when sung.

It is also often parodied. The most famous is in Lewis Carroll *Alice's Adventures in Wonderland* when the Mad Hatter says, "Twinkle, twinkle little bat! How I wonder what you're at! Up above the world you fly, Like a tea-tray in the sky." This nonsense actually refers to an Oxford math professor nicknamed "Bat" whose lectures soared way over the heads of his students.

CHAPTER EIGHT

Mother Goose Rhymes as Literature

References to Mother Goose rhymes have appeared in cartoons, news articles, and advertisements since they originated, for the most part over 200 years ago. From 1981 to 1997, for example, "The New Yorker" magazine had over thirty-five cartoons and front covers referring to characters and lines from the rhymes—"Humpty Dumpty" and "Hey Diddle Diddle" being the most frequent subjects.

Famous writers such as Lewis Carroll, the Pulitzer Prize winning novelist Robert Penn Warren, and contemporary writer Eve Merriman and others have used "Humpty Dumpty," " Sing a Song of Sixpence," and other Mother Goose figures and situations in their work.

It may seem difficult to believe, however, that these seemingly little nonsense ditties are "literature." "Jack and Jill" might seem, at first glance, like a little musical jingle to please babies.

However, a closer examination of these tiny poems shows that they are indeed, as poet Walter de la Mare has said, "tiny gems of word craftmanship." Using "Jack and Jill" as a prototype, one sees hallmarks of excellent literature that cause poet Robert Graves to believe that many Mother Goose rhymes are better than most of the verses in *The Oxford Dictionary of Light Verse*. A definition of good poetry is "the best words in the right order." "Jack and Jill" uses just the right words. And each word contributes to the telling of this dramatic little story that in six short lines has a beginning, middle, and ending—a conflict and resolution.

The words used are simple, fresh, and unselfconsciously poetic. The names, Jack and Jill, are musical both beginning with the letter J, using the technique of alliteration. These musical names start the rhyme right off with just the right bouncy lilt. The word "fetch" is economical. In one short word it describes both getting and bringing back the bucket of water.

The best verse uses unexpected rhyming words. Crown is an unusual word to rhyme with down. It is also comical, specifically describing the exact spot on the head that is hit. The use of "hill" to rhyme with "Jill" isn't unusual, but it isn't just put there to rhyme. It advances the action of the story. "Water" would be an unusual word to rhyme with "after," which it did in the 17th century when the rhyme was composed.

"Tumbling," of course, is a wonderful word describing Jill's fall. Using the technique of onomatopoeia, the word sounds like the action it describes, connoting both the clumsy and yet youthfully buoyant aspect of a child's fall.

The action of "Jack and Jill" has a magical quality. People don't ordinarily go up hills for water making this adventure unique and a little extraordinary.

As in all good literature, the ending of "Jack and Jill" is believable but a little unpredictable. In a jingle for children, we might expect that the little pair would skip happily up and then come happily down the hill with their bucket full of water. The fact that the couple tumble and fall is unexpected and somewhat unsettling.

This unsettling aspect of many Mother Goose rhymes has caused some critics (even since the days when the rhymes were first told to children) to want to ban them or substitute happy endings. Changing endings, of course, creates poems that are not the ones that have withstood the test of time or as Russian poet and critic Kornei Chukovsky once said, "have been sifted through a thousand sieves by the children so that only the best ones and the best language have survived."

It is a fact that the rhymes are sometimes unsettling. One woman, for example, recalls how, as a child, she felt uneasy by the spider in Miss Muffet and even the mouse scared by the clock in "Hickory, Dickory, Dock," but that she liked the poems, too. Psychologist-author Jack Sanford believes children like the poems despite their troubling aspect because they intuitively know the world is a scary place and that bad things happen sometimes. Indeed, as in all excellent literature and art of any kind, the rhymes express a truth. They are made enjoyable because they are poetically musical with rhythm and rhyme.

Indeed, a major function of literature is catharsis or giving the reader, listener, or actor the chance to experience feelings and emotions (both pleasant and unpleasant) without directly suffering the consequences. Catharsis has a positive psychological function making us realize we are all members of the human family and are not alone in our experiences of pleasure, struggle, and pain. Dramatizing the rhymes together and discussing them intensifies this feeling of a shared humanity because the participants are directly experiencing the characters' dilemmas and triumphs.

Young children particularly enjoy speculating on how the characters got into their unfortunate situations and how they felt when it happened. For example, when kindergarten students were asked why Jack fell down the hill, one said he caught his foot on a rock and yelled, "Oh, no!" Another said that the hill was too high, and he tripped. A third said that the reason Jill fell too was because she bumped into Jack.

When asked why Humpty Dumpty fell off of the wall, one girl said, "Someone pushed him." Speculating on the character's feelings and the cause of events, of course, develops both critical thinking and the imagination. A discussion of some of the "bad things that happen to the characters" even teaches safety in an non-didactic way, pointing out that we all must be careful in some circumstances in life.

Excellent literature is typified by memorable characters who are both universal types with whom we can identify and also unique individuals. The names Jack and Jill were synonymous with lass and lad in the 7th century. But we also feel this is a unique little couple. There has never been another pair going up a hill for water and then coming down in quite such a fashion.

And what of some other characters? Was there ever a maiden as tremulous as Miss Muffet, a king as jovial as King Cole, a boy quite as nimble as Jack, or a dog owner as solicitous as Old Mother Hubbard. And last and most outstanding is the figure of Humpty Dumpty, whom Jack Sanford calls, "a genius of the imagination."

A down-to-earth measure of a literature's greatness is how well it wears. Can the reader or reciter repeat it over and over again and still find it captivating? For generations, both children and adults have recited Mother Goose rhymes. Yearly, six or seven new picture books are published and many other resource materials based on the rhymes. Artists continue to want to illustrate them. Young people of all ages are eager to try their hand at illustrating them too.

As the title page of an 1843 book, *The Only True Mother Goose Melodies,* says:

"No, no, my Melodies will never die,
While nurses sing or babies cry."

And, may we add, as long as the imagination is free to fly!

CHAPTER NINE

Literature and History Questions and Research

Mother Goose rhymes illustrate literary conventions used in poetry. Many are tiny stories with lively characters, a beginning, middle, and ending and a dramatic conflict. Integrating a rhyme's history in a discussion deepens the appreciation of these remarkable poems.

Some of the following questions can be used with all students. Others are geared to upper grade and gifted students. Many can be adapted for use with different ages and abilities.

GENERAL LITERATURE, HISTORY, AND LANGUAGE ACTIVITIES

1. Mother Goose rhymes have lasted more than 200 years. Why do people continue to like them after all this time?
2. Former Poet Laureate Rita Dove says poetry needs "the oral voice running through it," meaning poetry should not only be read but also spoken. Many people say that Mother Goose rhymes are fun to recite by themselves and as you read them in a book. Recite a Mother Goose rhyme. Why do they say that?
3. Students of all ages enjoy discussing the problems and conflicts of the characters in Mother Goose. Good comprehension questions may stem from the characters' problems. For example, "What unfortunate thing happened to Humpty Dumpty, Miss Muffet, Bo-Peep, Old Mother Hubbard's dog, the robin in "The North Wind," the mouse who went up the clock, or Jack and Jill? How did the individual characters feel when they had their problems?
4. Students can learn the concept of beginning, middle, and ending events in a story or scene from these poems. For example, ask what was Jack Horner doing in the beginning, middle, and ending of his poem? Or, what did King Cole "call for" in the beginning, middle, and ending of his scene? Or, who was the first, middle, and last person to ask Baa, Baa, Black Sheep for wool?
5. Defining unknown words in a poem clarifies its meaning. Learning new words, of course, develops vocabulary and a love for language. To involve

students, let them guess a word's meaning from the roots (i.e. sixpence) or the context, "Jack be nimble," and then, check the meaning in a dictionary.

Some words in the poems to define are rye, parlor, dame, fetch, contrary, cockle shells, merry, cupboard, and curds and whey. Students benefit from discovering that "tuffet," "Hey, Diddle, Diddle," and "Hickory, Dickory, Dock" are made-up words and discussing why the poet used those words in the verse.

6. Introducing the class to a rhyme's history gives students a deeper appreciation of its meaning and a background on the history of the times. For example, (using Chapter Seven, "The History of Mother Goose Rhymes,") read the history of "Jack be Nimble" to learn why the boy leaped over a candle rather than another object. Study the history of Humpty Dumpty to learn how illustrators knew to depict him as an egg when his anatomy is never mentioned in the poem. Read the background on Old Mother Hubbard to discover how a young woman defied her brother to write one of the most popular poems of her times.

CULTURAL LITERACY QUESTION GAME

A way to help students learn the poems well is to play a "Name That Rhyme" TV game. In the game, the TV host (either the teacher or a student) gives contestants information from a rhyme, and the contestants tell which rhyme has that information.

Questions might be factual such as, "Which rhyme has a girl who lost a sheep?" They might be more subtle, such as, "Which has silverware?" Perhaps they might even infer characters' feelings, such as, "Which rhyme has a dissatisfied dog, an anxious girl, a haughty queen, an athletic boy?" Students, of course, benefit from creating the questions themselves.

DEVELOPING LANGUAGE QUESTIONS

1. Some people say students should not study Mother Goose because the rhymes use words like "fetch," "nimble," and "twinkle," and we don't use those kinds of words every day. Others say it's good to learn and to use unusual words. What do you think? Explain.
2. Many believe that in poems, more than in stories or novels, "every word must count." Recite a Mother Goose rhyme. What does it mean that every word in the poem must count?

POETIC LANGUAGE CONVENTION ACTIVITIES

Poets enjoy language. They often use words with certain sounds to make them fun to say and to help them describe the feeling they want to convey. The following describes some ways poets use the sounds of words to create musical effects.

1. Mother Goose rhymes often use ALLITERATION, or the repetition of an initial consonant sound in words that are close together. What three words in the phrase "Sing a Song of Sixpence" begin with the same consonant sound? What words in "Little Boy Blue Come Blow Your Horn" begin with the same consonant sound?

2. Alliteration is one of the oldest devices of English poetry. Say the phrase, "Sing a Song of Sixpence," and now say, "Little Boy Blue Come Blow Your Horn." Why do people enjoy these repeated sounds?

3. Sometimes writers make up characters whose first and last names begin with the same consonant. Such names as Black Beauty, Minnie Mouse, Peter Pan, Betty Boop, Miss Marple and Nicholas Nickleby use alliteration. Say these names. Why do you think writers make up characters with names beginning with the same letter?

4. Many Mother Goose rhymes have characters whose first and last names begin with the same letter. Look in Mother Goose books and find characters whose first and last names begin with the same letter. Say their names out loud.

5. Make up a boy's or girl's name whose first, last, and perhaps even middle names begin with the same consonant. Say the name out loud.

6. "Sing a Song of Sixpence" uses alliteration in its first line. "Wonderful Wobbly Watermelon," "Marvelous Melanie Muffins," and "Quirky Quarreling Quarter" are all phrases beginning with the same consonant. Make up a phrase that makes sense or is nonsense in which three words begin with the letter T. Say the phrase out loud.

7. ONOMATOPOEIA means using words that sound like the thing they describe. For example, "mumble" sounds like a person mumbling; "squeak" sounds like a squeaking mouse; "wiggle" sounds like something wiggling. Animal-sound words such as "Woof" and "Cluck, Cluck" resemble the sounds the animals make. Sound-effect words such as Boom!, Crash! and Whee! also use onomatopoeia. Which Mother Goose rhymes in this and other books use sound-effect words that sound like, or almost like, the sound they describe?

PLAYING WITH LANGUAGE

Cartoonists use sound-effect words such as "WOW!" for excitement, "WHOSH" for a wind, or "BOING" for a high leap. Sometimes they make up sound-effect words to create the sound of something that hasn't been described before. For example, a cat caught in a trash barrel might make a "FWAP" against the side, or a person biting into a lemon might say, "GLEEP!" Make up a sound-effect word for someone trying to push a rock up a hill; for the sound of dropping a glass on concrete; for the feeling of biting into icy cold ice cream.

RHYTHM AND RHYME

1. Mother Goose rhymes have a strong rhythm making them fun to recite. Recite "Hickory, Dickory, Dock" and tap the beat with the back of a pencil on your desk. Recite "Humpty Dumpty" and beat the rhythm with the palm of your hand against your desk or your knees.
2. Repeated words or phrases can create a rhythmic effect. Recite "Baa, Baa, Black Sheep." What words or phrases are repeated to create a kind of rhythm? Answer the same question after you recite each of the following rhymes: "Hickory, Dickory, Dock," "Oh, The Grand Old Duke of York," "Old King Cole," and "The North Wind Doth Blow."

Why are Mother Goose rhymes called rhymes? Recite a Mother Goose rhyme. What makes the poem rhyme? Why do people like rhymes? Why do the words that rhyme help people to memorize the rhyme?

MOTHER GOOSE AS NONSENSE VERSE

1. Many Mother Goose rhymes are nonsense verses. Nonsense verse is also called light verse. Why isn't it called heavy verse? What do you think is light about it?
2. Nonsense verse often has unusual things happen that probably couldn't happen in real life. "Hey Diddle, Diddle" is the most well-known nonsense poem in English. What unusual things happen in the poem? Why do people like nonsense verse even though it may not make sense?
3. Nonsense writers like to create imaginary characters. Humpty Dumpty is such a creation. What's strange about Humpty Dumpty? Say his name out loud. Does it sound right for the character? Explain.

4. Make up a nonsense character. Draw a picture of her or him. Give the character a name. Use a cartoon bubble and make up something the character says. Underneath your picture, write what's unusual about your character.

5. Nonsense writers often make up new words. The words describe something that has never been described before. Or, sometimes the nonsense word simply rhymes with the line above it. What made-up word is in "Little Miss Muffet?" What "made-up" sound-effects words are in the poem with the mouse running up the clock?

6. Dennis Lee, Shel Silverstein, Sheree Fitch, and Jack Prelutsky are modern nonsense poets. Find one of their (or another poet's) nonsense poems that you like and recite it to the class. What do you like about it? Is the poem similar in any way to a Mother Goose rhyme? Explain. How is it different? Do you think the poet you chose ever read Mother Goose rhymes? Explain.

THE LYRIC POEMS OF MOTHER GOOSE

Some Mother Goose rhymes are lyrics or song-like poems. They are not funny poems but have a lilting musical quality. In Ancient Greece, these poems were accompanied by the playing of a lyre, a musical instrument similar to a little harp, and the reason for the name, "lyric." Which Mother Goose rhymes in this and other books are lyrical? Do you like lyrical poems? Explain.

MOTHER GOOSE AS ART

1. Many artists have illustrated Mother Goose rhyme books since the rhymes were first published over 200 years ago. Artist today still want to illustrate them. Why do you think so many artists for so many years have wanted to illustrate the rhymes?

2. Illustrate one or more of your favorite Mother Goose rhymes. Perhaps draw it as a story—showing what is happening in the beginning, middle, and ending of the rhyme.

MOTHER GOOSE RHYMES TO RECITE, TO DRAMATIZE, AND TO PANTOMIME IN PAIRS AND GROUPS

1.
Baa, baa, black sheep,
   Have you any wool?
Yes, sir, yes, sir,
   Three bags full;
One for my master,
   One for my dame,
And one for the little boy
   Who lives down the lane.

2.
Hey! Diddle, diddle,
The cat and the fiddle,
The cow jumped over the moon;
The little dog laughed
To see such sport,
And the dish ran away with the spoon.

3.
Hickory, dickory, dock,
The mouse ran up the clock.
   The clock struck one.
   The mouse ran down.
Hickory, dickory, dock.

4.
Humpty Dumpty sat on a wall,
Humpty Dumpty had a great fall.
   All the king's horses
   And all the king's men,
Couldn't put Humpty together again.

5.
Jack and Jill went up the hill
   To fetch a pail of water;
Jack fell down and broke his crown,
   And Jill came tumbling after.

6.
Jack be nimble,
Jack be quick,
Jack jump over
The candlestick.

7.
Little Bo-Beep has lost her sheep,
   And doesn't know where to find them;
Leave them alone, and they'll come home,
   Wagging their tails behind them.

8.
Little Boy Blue
   Come blow your horn,
The sheep's in the meadow,
   The cow's in the corn;
But where is the boy
   Who looks after the sheep?
He's under a haystack
   Fast asleep.

Dramatizing Mother Goose

9.

Little Jack Horner
Sat in a corner,
Eating his Christmas pie;
He put in his thumb,
And pulled out a plum,
And said, "What a good boy am I!"

10.

Little Miss Muffet
Sat on a tuffet
Eating her curds and whey;
Along came a spider,
Who sat down beside her,
And frightened Miss Muffet away.

11.

Mary, Mary, quite contrary,
How does your garden grow?
With silverbells and cockle shells,
And pretty maids all in a row.

12.

The north wind doth blow,
And we shall have snow,
And what will poor robin do then?
    The poor thing!
He'll sit in a barn,
And to keep himself warm,
He'll hide his head under his wing.
    The poor thing!

13.

Oh, the grand old Duke of York,
    He had ten thousand men;
He marched them up to the top of the hill,
    And he marched them down again.
And when they were up, they were up,
    And when they were down, they were
        down,
And when they were only halfway up,
    There were neither up nor down.

14.

Old King Cole
Was a merry old soul,
And a merry old soul was he;
    He called for his pipe,
    And he called for his bowl,
And he called for his fiddlers three.
Tweedle dee, tweedle dee, tweedle dee,
    tweedle dee,
    Tweedle dee went the fiddlers three.

15.

Old Mother Hubbard
Went to the cupboard,
To fetch her poor dog a bone.
    But when she got there,
    The cupboard was bare,
And so the poor dog had none.

16.

Sing a song of sixpence,
A pocket full of rye;
Four and twenty blackbirds
Baked in a pie.

When the pie was opened,
The birds began to sing;
Wasn't that a dainty dish,
To set before the King?

The King was in his counting-house,
Counting out his money;
The queen was in the parlor,
Eating bread and honey.

The maid was in the garden,
Hanging out the clothes,
When along came a blackbird,
And pecked off her nose.
But then came a jenny wren,
Who popped it on again.

17.
Twinkle, twinkle, little star,
How I wonder what you are!
Up above the world so high,
Like a diamond in the sky,
Twinkle, twinkle, little star.
How I wonder what you are!

*When the blazing sun is gone,
When he nothing shines upon,
Then you show your little light,
Twinkle, twinkle, all the night.

Then the traveler in the dark,
Thanks you for your tiny spark,
He could not see which way to go,
If you did not twinkle so.

* *These verses are not dramatized in the book, but would be enjoyable to try.*

ACTIVITY LEVEL INDEX

QUIETING

MODERATELY ACTIVE

ACTIVE

Rhymes marked with * are listed in *The Dictionary of Cultural Literacy—What Every American Needs to Know* by E. D. Hirsch, Jr., et al. The other Mother Goose rhymes listed in *The Dictionary of Cultural Literacy* are "Jack Sprat," "Ride a Cock-Horse," "Ring around the Rosie," "Simple Simon," and "Three Blind Mice."

SUBJECT INDEX—MOTHER GOOSE ACROSS THE CURRICULUM

BIBLIOGRAPHY

The following books can provide useful resource material to enhance the learning experience for students and teachers. Books are listed according to category for ease of use.

MOTHER GOOSE PICTURE BOOKS

Sutherland, Zena, editor. *The Orchard Book of Nursery Rhymes.* Illustrated by Faith Jaques. Orchard Books, 1990. Charming illustrations of characters in English settings and 18th century costumes reflecting the setting and time when many rhymes were composed.

Langley, Jonathan, illustrator. *Rain, Rain Go Away!—A Book of Nursery Rhymes.* Dial Books for Young Readers, 1991. Exuberant whimsical illustrations that will appeal to all age levels.

Edens, Cooper, editor. *The Glorious Mother Goose.* Macmillan, 1988. Forty-two rhymes illustrated by late 19th and early 20th century artists such as Leslie Brooke, Randolph Caldecott, and Kate Greenaway. Develops art appreciation and an awareness of the unique styles of artists. Excellent to motivate students to create their own art.

Lobel, Arnold, illustrator. *The Random House Book of Mother Goose,* 1986. Imaginative illustrations of 306 rhymes by a Caldecott award winning illustrator. Includes all of the original verses of "Jack and Jill," "Little Bo-Peep," and "Old Mother Hubbard." A complete picture book anthology of Mother Goose rhymes.

Grove, Eulalie Osgood. *Mother Goose, The Classic Volland Edition.* Illustrated by Frederick Richardson, 1985. A classic book, first published in 1915, with over 300 rhymes. The appealing nostalgic watercolor illustrations in period costumes draw the viewer into another era.

DePaola, Tomie, illustrator. *Tomie de Paola's Mother Goose.* Putnam's, 1985. Simple, pleasant drawings with a sweet innocence appealing to young children.

SCHOLARLY AND HISTORICAL BOOKS

Delamar, Gloria T. *Mother Goose From Nursery to Literature*. McFarland and Company, Inc. Jefferson, North Carolina, 1987. A valuable and enjoyable book with chapters on the history of Mother Goose and the rhymes. Discusses the rhymes as literature, and writers and others who have borrowed material from them.

Opie, Iona and Peter. *The Oxford Dictionary of Nursery Rhymes*. Oxford University Press, 1951. The most thoroughly researched book on the origin of 550 rhymes. The Opies spent ten years researching this fascinating book that will be of interest to gifted and older students (grades five and above).

Hirsch, E. D. Jr., Joseph F. Kett, and James Trefil. *The Dictionary of Cultural Literacy—What Every American Needs to Know*. Houghton Mifflin, Boston, 1993. Describes historical and literary and other references Americans should know to be considered culturally literate and includes twenty Mother Goose rhymes. A provocative, helpful reference for teachers and parents.

OTHER MOTHER GOOSE RESOURCES

Mother Goose Guild News. Joanne Ladd, editor. Twice-yearly newsletter devoted to resources and Mother Goose events throughout the country. Cost is "one dollar every once in awhile" to cover postage, according to the editor, Joanne Ladd, who is herself a "Mother Goose." 1406 Kettering Road, Burton, MI 48509.

CREATING SIMPLE COSTUMES

Cummings, Richard. *101 Costumes for All Ages, All Occasions*. Boston: Plays, Inc., 1987. Cleverly illustrated suggestions on how to adapt clothes and make simple costumes for all cultures and historical periods.

MUSICAL INSTRUMENTS AND SOUND EFFECTS

West Music Company, 1208 5th Street, Coralville, IA 52241 (1-800-397-9378) A very complete catalogue of reasonably priced instruments from many cultures. Includes books on teaching music and movement, helpful in dramatizing the rhymes in this book.

Wiseman, Ann. *Making Musical Things*. New York: Charles Scribner's Sons, 1979. Simple instruments made of kitchen utensils, pieces of wood, pipe, and other ordinary things.

Cook, Wayne. *Center Stage, A Curriculum for the Performing Arts*. Menlo Park, CA: Dale Seymour Publications, 1993. Two-volume curriculum with 30 sequential lessons for each grade from kindergarten to grade six. One volume is for kindergarten through third grade, and a second covers grades four through six.

Gerke, Pamela and Landalf, Helen, *Movement Stories for Children Ages 3–6*. Lyme, NH: Smith and Kraus, 1996. Detailed discussion on the importance of movement in children's development and a helpful explanation of movement concepts with ten active stories to be narrated for children to act.

Thistle, Louise. *Dramatizing Aesop's Fables*. Menlo Park, CA: Dale Seymour Publications, 1993. Aesop's Fables dramatized for the classroom or use on the stage. Includes acting techniques, character warm-ups, and critical thinking questions.

Thistle, Louise. *Dramatizing the Little Red Hen* and *Dramatizing the Lion and the Mouse*. Lectorum Publications Inc., 1996. Dramatic action picture books (available in English and Spanish) with pictures and chants to act every sentence in each story. Recommended for teachers of English learners and children preschool to grade three.

Thistle, Louise. *Dramatizing Myths and Tales*. Menlo Park, CA: Dale Seymour Publications, 1995. Myths and tales dramatized from five cultures—West African, Mayan, Native American, Japanese, and English. Written to give all students a significant role. Includes critical thinking and research questions. Describes how to dramatize the myths on stage and in the classroom.